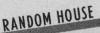
RANDOM HOUSE

Winter Treat
crosswords

edited by **Stanley Newman**

Random House
Puzzles & Games

NEW YORK   TORONTO   LONDON   SYDNEY   AUCKLAND

P9-CBT-816

Introduction

Welcome to Random House Winter Treat Crosswords, with 100 light and breezy puzzles from some of America's most talented puzzle-makers. Each crossword has a theme, or central idea, running through its longest answers. The title provided at the top of each page will give you a hint as to what the theme is. And the answers are all in the back, just in case.

Thanks to Sandy Fein and Greg Pliska for their help in the preparation of the manuscript.

Your comments on any aspect of this book are most welcome. You can reach me via regular mail or e-mail at the addresses below.

If you're Internet-active, you're invited to my Web site, www .StanXwords.com. It features puzzlemaker profiles, solving hints and other useful info for crossword fans. There's also a free daily crossword and weekly prize contest. Please stop by for a visit.

Best wishes for happy solving!

Stan Newman

Regular mail: P.O. Box 69, Massapequa Park, NY 11762
(Please enclose a self-addressed stamped envelope if you'd like a reply.)

E-mail: StanXwords@aol.com

Join Stan Newman on His Annual Crossword-Theme Cruise!

You'll enjoy a relaxing vacation on a luxurious ship, plus a full program of puzzles, games and instructional sessions. For complete info on Stan's next cruise, please phone Special Event Cruises at 1-800-326-0373, or visit their Web site, www.specialeventcruises.com/crossword.html.

1 REED IT AND WEEP

. . . .

by A.J. Santora

ACROSS

1 Fannie __
4 Injury
8 Do a knee jerk
13 Invoice
14 Mixture
15 Grouch of TV
16 START OF A DEFINITION OF AN OBOE
18 Domingo's domain
19 __ U.S. Pat. Off.
20 Copier chemicals
22 The youngest Cratchit
23 Metaphysical poet John
25 Tender
26 Prosperous period
27 Bread spread
28 Prepayment
30 Ankle-related
33 Heavenly
34 MIDDLE OF DEFINITION
36 Accounts-payable stamp
39 Bookstore statistic
43 Emergency force
44 Drink too much
45 Mouth-to-mouth
46 Jazzman Getz
49 Elementary computer language
50 Squeal

51 Beret, e.g.
53 Nationality suffix
54 Job for an emcee
56 END OF DEFINITION
58 The flock
59 Musical Horne
60 Hosiery shade
61 Past the deadline
62 Snappish?
63 Western Amerind

DOWN

1 Big Apple suburb
2 Straight man?
3 Kay follower
4 "__ I doin'?": Ed Koch
5 Alternative name
6 Beatle with the sticks
7 Faster than andante
8 Aussie jumpers
9 Predictive power, initially
10 Paint solvent
11 *Flying Down to Rio* dance
12 Restrain
13 . . . *And God Created Woman* star
17 Golf ball position
21 Frank
24 Little breather
26 Robert Blake TV role
29 Start of Caesar's boast

31 "There'll be ___
time . . ."
32 Extravagant
33 Cut off
35 Service support?
36 Lover of love
37 Dangerous swimmer
38 Lunch order
40 Miss an opportunity

41 Serial part
42 Withdraw
47 Cop ___
48 Nitery lights
49 Kramden's workplace
51 Reproduce
52 Out of here
55 Embarrassed
57 Antelope type

2 WHOOPS!

by Shirley Soloway

ACROSS

1 Voice-master Mel
6 Venomous snakes
10 Pro __ (proportionally)
14 Farmlike
15 Card game
16 Adam Arkin's dad
17 Having hard times
19 Abel's brother
20 Tiny
21 Coral deposit
22 Airplane walkway
23 Jackpots
26 Storage areas
29 Strong singers
33 Church seats
34 Tour of duty
36 i topper
37 Vocal gaffe
41 Overhead trains
42 Skin openings
43 __ of Eden
44 Fill up
46 Moms of Madrid
48 TV-image defects
51 Western ties
54 Fem. opposite
55 Model Carol
58 Baseball manager Felipe
59 Heavy tool
62 Bridle control
63 Voice range
64 *Lorna __*
65 Bank purchase
66 Onetime atlas initials
67 School assignment

DOWN

1 Eye topper
2 *"Clair de __"*
3 Johnson of comedy
4 Slangy refusal
5 Man of the cloth
6 Made a request
7 Sailing ship
8 Cushion
9 Ave. crossers
10 Archie Bunker, e.g.
11 "Too bad!"
12 Kite appendage
13 Actress Bancroft
18 Capitol VIPs
22 __ the good (desirable)
23 Thin streak
24 __ *Irish Rose*
25 Pre-Easter season
26 Church recesses
27 "I cannot __ lie"
28 Entwine
30 Bergen or Poe
31 Wake up
32 Editors' marks
34 Type of germ, for short
35 One article
38 Semiprecious stones

39 Snapshot, in product names
40 Sparks and Beatty
45 "Blueberry Hill" opener
46 Openwork fabric
47 Mall area
49 Fails to include
50 Kettle output
51 Fence defense

52 Bread spread
53 Beef cut
55 Cookie king
56 Olin or Horne
57 Low card
59 Sigma follower
60 *Treasure Island* monogram
61 Parts of yrs.

3 INTEMPERANCE

by Randolph Ross

ACROSS

1 USN rank
4 Thom of shoedom
8 Peer
13 Talk like Fudd
15 Mobil competitor
16 Reach, as a total
17 Word form for "Mars"
18 Impolite look
19 Dangerous gas
20 Fusspot
22 Synthetic materials
23 Intemperate vegetables?
25 Batting failures
26 Eva's half-sister?
27 What *le* means
30 Yell
33 Opposite of post-
34 Pants unit
35 Intemperate entrée?
39 Unwelcome picnic guests
40 Brain-wave picture: Abbr.
41 Broad neckwear
42 Ref's call, for short
43 E.T. craft
44 "Who __?" (doorbell response)
46 Intemperate fruit?
51 Treacher or Miller
54 Star's part

55 Doctor, at times
56 Happy
57 Author Hunter
58 Noncitizen
59 Head of France
60 Match divisions
61 High-school books
62 Wallet fillers
63 Golfer Trevino

DOWN

1 Envelope device
2 Serial opener
3 Fatty acid
4 Barrel-headed hammer
5 Sets of beliefs
6 Sour
7 Hide-hair connector
8 Publishing problems
9 Piers
10 Disassemble
11 Like __ of bricks
12 Chaney and Nol
14 Anti-labor actions
21 Jane Fonda film
22 Bowler's button
24 Poet Pound
27 After-bath application
28 Hawaiian port
29 Prefix for while
30 Quarrel
31 Goose greeting

32 Palindromic name
33 Cribbage piece
34 Cow-feterias?
36 Put off
37 Cat call
38 Puppeteer Bil
43 Reversals of a sort
44 Conceptualize
45 A suit

46 Piece of paper
47 Barkin or Burstyn
48 Innovative
49 Bring joy to
50 Logic
51 ". . . to skin __"
52 Reign
53 Kids' cereal
56 Beach Boys' car

4 WHODUNIT HIT
by Cynthia Lyon

ACROSS

1 Does logging
5 __ off (occasionally)
10 __ *Lap* ('83 film)
14 Touched the turf
15 Tijuana title
16 Herbert Hoover's birthplace
17 A little force?
18 Open boat
19 Icky terrain
20 THE ACTRESS
23 Traditional stuff
24 Take to court
25 Western shows
28 Actor Sharif
30 Holemaker
33 Make a statement
34 Sea cells
35 Sudden start
36 THE ROLE
40 Be a thorn
41 Desiccated
42 Dog owner's shout
43 Duct
44 Carson's successor
45 __ *From a Marriage*
47 Suite piece
48 Emmy winner, maybe
49 THE SHOW
56 Prefix meaning "billionth"
57 "Never!"
58 Religious symbol
59 Sartre's *No __*
60 Democratic Republic of the Congo, once
61 Have coming
62 Alongside of
63 Set for a skirmish
64 Last word of the year?

DOWN

1 Actress Thompson
2 Kirk __ (a film Superman)
3 Buck's partner
4 Pittsburgh pro team
5 Hepburn's quartet
6 Tennis pro Fraser
7 __ *Karenina*
8 Lunch time, often
9 Equestrian exhibition
10 Vexed feeling
11 Lunch time, often
12 On the road
13 Joplin piece
21 Card game
22 Popped
25 Indira's son/successor
26 __ barrel (helpless)
27 Office furniture
28 Gluck role
29 Springlike
30 White, in a way
31 A question of location

32 Old-time strings
34 TV's Barbara or Conrad
37 Didn't work
38 Legless sideboard
39 Slot-machine fruits
45 Beyond tipsy
46 Blackbird's comment
47 Soup base

48 Seaside
49 Long skirt
50 Troop group
51 React to a riot?
52 Wedge
53 Authorize
54 Ripped
55 Feminine suffix
56 Inexperienced

ACROSS

1 *The Planets* composer
6 Musante role
10 Pin kin
14 Wife of Prince Valiant
15 Deserter's status
16 Coin of Iran
17 Surgical tool
18 Send back to Congress
19 Economist Smith
20 Not quite an all-star
23 Writer Wiesel
24 Praise
25 Indy 500 time
27 Breathing sound
30 Mechanical pieces
33 Work unit
34 *Billy Budd* character
35 Jobs around
   the house
37 Not quite magic
40 Most angry
41 Rayburn or
   Roddenberry
42 Coffeepot
43 Fernando and Aldo
44 Ubangi tributary
45 *Emerald Point* ___ (TV
   series)
46 Pile
48 Anti-DWI org.
51 Not quite real
   happiness

56 Suave
57 A dimension
58 Whopper
60 Mist
61 Man with a lift
62 Become accustomed (to)
63 Iowa city
64 Nikita's negative
65 Coup ___

DOWN

1 Linden of *The Boys
   Are Back*
2 Norwegian name
3 "Judy's Turn To Cry"
   singer
4 Shoplift
5 Foot bones
6 "Rikki-Tikki-___"
7 Author Wister
8 Mark with spots
9 Wahine's hello
10 Stage exit
11 Operatic slave
12 *For the Boys* star
13 Dutch airline
21 Because of this
22 Game with a
   five-card hand
25 Service chow
26 Iron clothing
28 Son of 14 Across
29 Pigeon's landing site

31 Hits an infield one-hopper, perhaps
32 Missionary Junipero
34 Container
35 The movies
36 9-digit IDs: Abbr.
38 Sites for snoopers
39 Tillis or Tormé
44 Snobbish
47 __ Martin (007's auto)

49 Extra
50 One of Saturn's satellites
51 Pillow filler
52 Move like The Blob
53 French confidante
54 Break
55 Biblical scribe
56 Dance syllable
59 As __ (so far)

6 TACTFULLY PUT

by Donna J. Stone

ACROSS

1 Coll. hotshot
5 *R.U.R.* dramatist
10 Samoa studier
14 Morning wear
15 '60s baseballer Tony
16 Part of TAE
17 "Alphabet Song" gamut
18 Flight segment
19 Simpleton
20 DIPLOMACY
DEFINITION: PART 1
23 Comedian Louis
24 Bone-dry
25 Scales of *Fawlty Towers*
30 Five iron
34 Stud site
35 *Shane* star
37 Martin and Stockwell
38 Flap
39 DEFINITION: PART 2
41 Circle
42 Pageant prop
44 Request
45 Raison d'___
46 Unexpurgated
48 Make a guess
50 Macadamize
52 Sleet, essentially
53 DEFINITION: PART 3
61 Rely (on)
62 Actor Alain
63 Tender
64 Palomino's pride
65 Soap star Slezak
66 Face shape
67 Floored it
68 Fortify
69 Foster film

DOWN

1 Wild child
2 Butterfly kin
3 Bassoon relative
4 Post-Impressionist painter
5 Singer Elvis
6 Countertenor
7 Chanteuse Edith
8 Ills
9 Big name in basketball
10 Toy terrier
11 Wells race
12 Revlon rival
13 "___ Me" (Roger Miller tune)
21 Bread or booze
22 Swap
25 Service member?
26 *The Kiss* sculptor
27 *Kapitän*'s command
28 Reader's need
29 Mr. Rochester's ward
31 "___ luego"

32 Motionless
33 Helena's competitor
36 *Bambi* extras
39 Miles or Purcell
40 Citizen
43 Aged
45 "The Sage of Concord"
47 Dodges
49 Hosp. area

51 Turn inside out
53 *Desire Under the __*
54 Bound
55 Sound
56 Nobelist Wiesel
57 Draft device
58 Emulated Arachne
59 Asian inland sea
60 Say "Hey!"

1	2	3	4		5	6	7	8	9		10	11	12	13
14					15						16			
17					18						19			
20				21						22				
			23					24						
25	26	27				28	29		30			31	32	33
34					35			36		37				
38				39					40			41		
42			43			44					45			
46				47		48			49					
			50			51			52					
53	54	55				56	57				58	59	60	
61				62						63				
64				65						66				
67				68						69				

7 COLORIZATION

by Bob Lubbers

ACROSS

1 Take down __
    (belittle)
5 Mad rush
9 Prefix for marine
    or sonic
14 Carson predecessor
15 Butter substitute
16 Master, in India
17 Dietrich film, with *The*
19 Take a whiff
20 Kind of vine
22 Stare at
23 Dispute decider
26 Hardened (to)
28 French port
29 Enticement
31 Stretch, as one's neck
32 Wave hello
33 Sup
36 Makes a tape: Abbr.
37 Terrific
38 Baxter or Boleyn
39 Ararat arrival
40 Three-note chord
41 Pistol provider
42 Puffs up
44 Rose oils
45 Hibernates
47 Eye parts
48 Afternoon parties
49 North Star
52 Awaken

54 Gary Cooper film of '28
58 Starts a pot
59 Moolah
60 Zest
61 Star of 32 Down
62 "__ sow, so shall . . ."
63 Go to __ (deteriorate)

DOWN

1 Police dept. radio
    message
2 Chum
3 __ de Cologne
4 Corinth citizens
5 Gift recipients
6 Writer Horatio __
7 Flow slowly
8 Golfer's target
9 Amer. vessel
    designation
10 Costar of Hope and
    Crosby
11 Sim film
12 Moon valley
13 Otherwise __
    (differently qualified)
18 Clarinetist Shaw
21 Signed a new tenant
23 Capital of Ghana
24 Less common
25 Horsy film of '46
27 Bolt fastener
29 Vicinities

30 Like a __ balloon
32 *True* __ ('69 western)
34 "It's the end of __"
35 Short and sweet
37 Hold, as a handrail
38 Performers
40 "You're the __" (Porter tune)
41 Storage space
43 Abate

44 Add fizz to
45 Malt-shop freebie
46 Hotelier Helmsley
47 Mass meeting
50 Gymnast Korbut
51 Is situated
53 Linguistic suffix
55 __ de France
56 West or Murray
57 Finish

8 *THE HARD STUFF*

by Robert H. Wolfe

ACROSS

1 Tracking system
6 Helper
10 TV overseer
13 Get out of bed
14 Eve or Enoch
15 __-di-dah
16 Music genre
18 Chemical suffix
19 NASA remark
20 Military memento, perhaps
21 Winter weather
22 Max Sr. and Jr.
23 *Altered* __ (William Hurt film)
25 Make the turkey even juicier
28 Finds fault
29 They matter in matter
30 Height or age, e.g.
34 Without a __ (broke)
35 Distress letters
36 Poetic form
37 Some joiners
41 Fiscal penalties
43 Sturdy carts
44 Solemn
46 Refrigerants
48 The Ram
49 Bring in
50 Dean Martin song subject
51 Undergraduate degs.
54 Relative of Inc.
55 California golf course
58 Grassland
59 U.S. Grant's foe
60 __ nous (confidentially)
61 Navy VIP
62 Unique person
63 Curves

DOWN

1 __ avis
2 Buck finisher
3 Powell or Cheney
4 Call (for)
5 Gather again
6 Wall hanging
7 Adored one
8 Neighbor of Penna.
9 Blow up a photo: Abbr.
10 Rubble's buddy
11 Lake craft
12 Masticates
14 Gives a talk
17 Nair rival
21 Lunkheads
22 Sound of impact
23 What Miss Muffet did
24 Three: Pref.
25 Demolish, in Devon
26 British school
27 Former Colorado River name

28 Baking dish
31 Little piggy
32 Bad day for Caesar
33 "___ la vie!"
38 Do a laundry chore
39 ___ Mateo, CA
40 Cobb and Hardin
41 Giveaway
42 Electees
45 Leeds' river
46 *The Most Happy ___*

47 Emulated Ebert
48 Yellowish
50 Competent
51 Belfry denizens
52 Farm measure
53 "___ a Lady"
(Tom Jones song)
55 Money player
56 Evening, to Noyes
57 Pulver's rank: Abbr.

9 BATMAN VILLAINS

by Dean Niles

ACROSS

1 Niger neighbor
5 Some snakes
9 Strikebreakers
14 Old __, CT
15 Rachel's sister
16 River embankment
17 Cassandra portrayer on *Batman*
19 Stage digression
20 Calendar abbr.
21 *Les* __(musical, for short)
22 Score intervals
24 Specialty periodicals
27 Poet's contraction
28 Oilcan letters
29 Make too much of
34 Pipe up
37 Sharp-tongued
38 "Fine by me!"
39 Crackerjack
40 Nongeneric swabs
41 Bog down
42 Hauteur
43 Colorado Indians
44 Dollar divisions
45 Felicitous
47 Controversial coat
48 Gloomy __
49 Like old paper
54 Crusades opponent
58 Once around
59 Govt. agency
60 Common people
61 The Archer portrayer on *Batman*
64 Tippy boat
65 Castle
66 Genesis place
67 Court decision
68 Pros and __
69 NASDAQ rival

DOWN

1 Clavin or Huxtable
2 Largest constellation
3 Full-force
4 __ Monte pineapple
5 Elevated
6 Take hold of
7 Bad notice
8 "Beat it!"
9 Actor Christian
10 The Joker portrayer on *Batman*
11 Tel __
12 Venerable monk
13 Calls on
18 Aleut craft
23 Dorm group
25 Minerva portrayer on *Batman*
26 Part of 54 Down
30 Mr. and Ms. Big
31 Related

32 Sour-tasting
33 Takes in
34 Cashless transaction
35 Donahue or Spector
36 Word on Irish coins
37 Memo opener
40 Resembling
44 *Mea* __
46 Made soap bubbles
47 Publicity seekers

50 First name in rock
51 Playwright Wasserstein
52 Fencing needs
53 Singer Taylor
54 Pet org.
55 "There oughta be __!"
56 Actress Olin
57 DEA agent
62 'Supial
63 Stimpy's pal

10 HOLY

by Fred Piscop

ACROSS

1 '30s boxing champ
5 Ignore
9 Contemptuous remark
14 Land measure
15 Actress Skye
16 It fell in 1836
17 Three holy items
20 Type of poem
21 TV scan lines
22 FedEx rival
23 Kind of tent
24 Place for a small house
25 Nincompoops
28 Change drastically
30 Bachelor's last words?
31 Add
32 Rio Grande city
36 Two holy items
40 Ace's home, perhaps
41 Actress Hagen
42 *Le __ Soleil*
43 Major meals
45 Ward off
47 Café au __
50 Dollar divs.
51 Foreman beater
52 Painter Maurice
54 Chemist Lavoisier
58 Five holy items
60 Monogram ltrs.
61 "Good Lord!"
62 __ *kleine Nachtmusik*
63 Not exactly brilliant
64 Take out
65 Frog kin

DOWN

1 Bases
2 Advil target
3 Cupid counterpart
4 Take it easy
5 Inks
6 Mrs. Charles
7 Actress Merkel
8 Mediterranean seaport
9 Handles clumsily
10 Female Oscar Madison
11 Bigoted one
12 "__ bagatelle!"
13 More severe
18 They come to those who wait?
19 California city
23 Stats for Mattingly
25 Letter starter
26 Graven image
27 Dermatologist's target
28 Comfy shoe
29 Greek letter
31 Oversweet sentimentality
33 De Valera's land
34 Portal
35 "Step __!"
37 Radicals of a sort

38 Arden of *Our Miss Brooks*
39 Rainier and others: Abbr.
44 Used the overhead
45 Meter starter
46 Part of Roy G. Biv
47 All there
48 Make reparation
49 Novelist Shaw

51 Battery terminal
53 __ majesty (sovereign crime)
54 What the suspicious smell
55 Word form for "personal"
56 Grandma
57 Took notice of
59 Turkish VIP

11

TOWN TALK
. . . .
by Michael Selinker

ACROSS
1 Ditty singer Doris
4 Gym surface
7 Vessel
10 A-E link
13 Binding words
14 Jeff Lynne's grp.
15 Actor Vigoda
16 Old high note
17 *Calamity Jane* ditty, part 1
21 Caliban's tormentor
22 Blind parts
23 Ditty, part 2
28 Ruckus
29 Bill's partner
30 Past
31 Shocking swimmer
32 Northumbrian's neighbor
34 Unique sorts
36 Ditty, part 3
41 Ancient Persians
42 *Guarding __* (MacLaine film)
45 Time
48 Buddy
49 Cub org.
52 Caviar source
53 Ditty, part 4
57 Caroline Islands group
58 Mountain ridge
59 Ditty, part 5

65 Ethiopian prince
66 Short word before "long"
67 Peace, to Akihito
68 Discovery cry
69 Superman's emblem
70 Mr. Spade
71 Program interruptors
72 Ditty, part 6

DOWN
1 Half of MIV
2 Dict. abbr.
3 "The sunshine of my life"
4 Measuring system
5 Inkless postage stamp
6 Klinger's hometown
7 Cat's dog
8 Kimono closer
9 About 100 feet high
10 Tongue-lash
11 Provide attire
12 Distressed one?
18 Called with chips
19 Tarzan player Ron
20 Soar
23 QB's stats
24 Sot's syllable
25 Archaic adverb
26 "Who __ Turn To?"
27 "__ no kick . . ."
33 Conway or Allen

34 Mil. training place
35 Tend the kids
37 ___ *Daughter* (Esther Williams film)
38 Normandy time
39 Squeal
40 Eastern European
43 Worthless coin
44 Collection
45 Ottoman's pride
46 Cow ropes
47 *Through ___, Darkly*

49 Howitzer sobriquet
50 Blotto
51 ___ time (now)
54 "Bali ___"
55 Gandhi successor
56 Affirmative vote
60 Musical syllable
61 Amethyst, e.g.
62 Touching game
63 *Tommy* group, with "The"
64 Chow down

12 THE CAMPBELLS

· · · · · · · · · · · · · · ·

by Bill Hendricks

ACROSS
1 Edition
6 Chan remark
10 Game-show VIP
14 Ten-___ odds
15 Hope/Crosby movie milieu
16 Sweet sandwich
17 Soup
20 Prefix meaning "whole"
21 "Kingly" name
22 Simoleons
23 Choose
25 "You're putting ___!"
26 Soup
31 Guess: Abbr.
34 Like Harvard walls
35 *The Good ___* (Buck book)
37 Altar constellation
39 Ling-Ling, e.g.
40 When lunch hour may end
41 Carpenter's garment
43 Bad deed
44 Approach dawn
46 First American-born saint
47 Sodium hydroxide
49 Soup
51 Layer
53 Klutz
54 Auto emporium
57 Use a +
59 '77 sea thriller
63 Soup
66 Start of Caesar's boast
67 Marsh grass
68 Get out of line
69 "Is You ___ Is You Ain't Ma Baby?"
70 Cravings
71 Turns on the waterworks

DOWN
1 Septennial affliction?
2 London neighborhood
3 Ground
4 Raw
5 "A mouse!"
6 "Rule Britannia" composer
7 Humbug
8 ___ Diego, CA
9 Leftover
10 It's funny
11 Vocal
12 Some vaccines
13 "Baloney!"
18 Art Deco artist
19 Jack of *Barney Miller*
24 Go biking
25 Leatherneck
26 Sharp barks
27 Benefit

28 Fool
29 "Scram!"
30 Ingested
32 Andrea del __
33 Scottish golf town
36 "__ la vista"
38 Ms. Meara
42 Necessarily
45 Lovey?
48 Cylindrical pastry
50 Repairs the lawn
52 __ pah pah

54 A quarter of DCCCXXIV
55 Warmonger of myth
56 "The Biggest Little City in the World"
57 Mass conclusion
58 Clothing
60 Learning method
61 Clever accomplishment
62 Rock-band equipment
64 Admission charge
65 Hem's partner

13 FOR GOOD MEASURE

by Shirley Soloway

ACROSS

1 Ice and Iron
5 Sky light?
9 Strong string
14 Pre-Easter season
15 Former Milan money
16 Duck down
17 "__ boy!"
18 Whale of a movie
19 Adds and deletes
20 Close call
23 TV sleuth
    Remington __
24 Arnold's crime
28 Small amount
31 Ed Norton's concern
32 Soviet news agency
35 Grain keeper
37 Indian tourist town
38 Curved opening
39 Squelch
40 __ over (faint)
41 Philippine native
42 Difficult
43 Matched pieces
44 Cook too much
46 Liffey's land
48 Work on an old
    painting, perhaps
50 Mrs. Marcos
55 Math subject
58 Thread holder
61 Actress Lollobrigida

62 Cozy
63 Golfer Palmer, to fans
64 Wicked
65 Border
66 Showy blossom
67 P.I.s
68 Satirist Mort

DOWN

1 Thicke and Bates
2 Reach
3 __ *nous*
4 Gaze intently
5 More leisurely
6 Grow weary
7 Circle segments
8 Show feeling
9 Indian abode
10 Very alert
11 General Amin
12 Court divider
13 Hosp. areas
21 Car maker
22 Fiery felony
25 Bob of *Full House*
26 Folklore villains
27 *Hud* actress
29 Europe's neighbor
30 British bishop's hat
32 Treasure find
33 *Green* __ (old sitcom)
34 Cut of meat
36 City near Sacramento

38 Latin love
39 Stripped of wool
43 Trucking rig
45 "Hang down your head, Tom __"
47 Adversaries
49 Urged (on)
51 Road curves

52 Evangelista or Evans
53 Unbaked bread
54 Jockey Cordero
56 Seedy establishment
57 "What's __ for me?"
58 Syrup source
59 Ante- kin
60 Mrs. Lennon

14 CLEAN UP YOUR ACT

by Ray Smith

ACROSS

1 __ Kadiddlehopper
5 Bloomingdale's rival
9 Pixyish
14 Mystic writing
15 Sight from the Strait of Messina
16 Mrs. Gorbachev
17 "Put __ on it!"
18 Energy source
19 Lubricated
20 Blues great
23 Numerical prefix
24 Producer Norman
25 More elevated
27 Nutria, e.g.
30 Down in the dumps
32 __ Amin
33 Smooth transition
35 Nostrils
38 "The __ From Ipanema"
40 Hits the fridge
42 Robert De __
43 Joins the game, in a way
45 __ du jour (daily specials)
47 Langley org.
48 Ran on
50 Former anchor of note
52 Clubs carrier
54 "__ to Love" (Porter song)
55 In the past
56 Crummy diner
62 Nonmusician's instrument
64 Leftovers category: Abbr.
65 Fascinated by
66 Happening
67 Toon's lightbulb
68 Defeats a bridge contract
69 Parking lot souvenirs
70 Speak wildly
71 Ilium

DOWN

1 Burn the midnight oil
2 "Little" cartoon character
3 Geraint's wife
4 Be a snoop
5 Brine
6 Rose oil
7 Slip or square item
8 "Ditto"
9 Wearing away
10 Chou En-__
11 More than well off
12 Grenoble's river
13 Low point
21 Urges

22 Letter after pi
26 Fed. agent
27 Baltic seaport
28 Asgard resident
29 Trini Lopez, Jim Brown, Ernest Borgnine, etc.
30 Craftsmen's group
31 Mother of Castor and Pollux
34 Stare in wonder
36 Eastern canal
37 Emulate Yeager
39 Coveted role
41 Pound denizen

44 Keg taps
46 Smart talk
49 Part of RPM
51 Office worker
52 Crusted
53 Century plant
54 Big Bertha's birthplace
57 Mideast title
58 Verdi heroine
59 Special person
60 Preminger or von Bismarck
61 Like a yenta
63 Mich. neighbor

15 BUTTERFINGERS

by Ann Seidel

ACROSS

1 Leno or Letterman
5 Misbehave
10 Whimpers
14 Opera highlight
15 Eighth Hebrew letter
16 Singer Laine
17 Beatles movie
18 Certain movie role
19 Be in charge of
20 Comics caveman
22 Bird claw
24 Insurance claim
25 __ to pass (occur)
26 Stay for the duration
29 Broadcast boo-boos
33 Shady recess
34 Excursions
35 Rim
36 Grate upon
37 Baby carriages
38 __-item veto
39 Enzyme suffix
40 Idaho capital
41 Loyal Order of __
42 Farm structures
44 Kicked (out)
45 Make a wish
46 Nurse in *Martin Chuzzlewit*
47 Piece of pottery
49 '50s fad
53 Potion container
54 Send by computer
56 Words of despair
57 Put out of commission
58 Popular lily
59 Half of CVI
60 Pizzazz
61 Struck, in a way
62 Ages upon ages

DOWN

1 "That's a laugh!"
2 Pitcher Hershiser
3 Window frame part
4 Replay mechanism
5 Confront
6 Total confusion
7 Office sub
8 Colorado Native American
9 Certain staged events
10 Lug around
11 Toast spread
12 Fiber source
13 Ground cover
21 "__ Cheatin' Heart"
23 Bible book
25 Weather, in poems
26 Beatrice's mother
27 Clean the blackboard
28 Actor Buddy
29 Military officers
30 Nobel poet
31 Wash cycle

32 Hightail it
34 Rubbish
37 Ship area
38 Way out
40 Rude, crude dude
41 NYC cultural attraction
43 Swiss cottage
44 "__ of the Green Berets"

46 Cunning treachery
47 "Them" or "us"
48 Holbrook and Linden
49 Fit as a fiddle
50 Buckeye State
51 From here __ (henceforth)
52 French veggies
53 That is to say, briefly
55 __ of La Mancha

16 NAP TIME

by Fred Piscop

ACROSS

1 Man with a touch
6 *Kidnapped* monogram
9 Sergeant Garcia's quarry
14 Put up with
15 Second-sequel indicator
16 Self-evident truth
17 Tacked
19 Rodeo rope
20 The two Begleys
21 Dash feature
22 Harmonica virtuoso Larry
23 Current strength
25 Pollute
29 Tom of *Newhart*
33 Darth Vader-like
34 Squirt
38 __-Wan Kenobi
39 Bandleader Prado
41 Prescription agcy.
42 Biblical brother
44 Lode stuff
45 Secret stuff
48 Restrain
49 Power of filmdom
51 Vixen's partner
53 Autocrats' realms
57 Prickly plants
60 Underworld
61 School grp.

64 Recovery process, for short
65 Oxygen converters
67 Battlefield
68 __ Bingle (Crosby)
69 Sources of irritation
70 Errand person
71 Western beast
72 Souvenir

DOWN

1 Pencil puzzle
2 Footnote abbr.
3 Pad
4 Wood shaper
5 *Hard to Kill* star
6 Construct haphazardly
7 Faithful
8 Partisan
9 City in España
10 Rust et al.
11 Iranian coin
12 Learning method
13 Barbra's costar in '68
18 Fun's partner
24 Prone
25 Bus station
26 "__ dog has his day"
27 Kiln operator
28 __ de France
30 Shul scroll
31 Amin deposed him

32 San Francisco footballer
35 Cpl.'s inferior
36 Dietary initials
37 Actor McShane
40 Big island
43 Pecs' partners
46 New Deal agcy.
47 Madison Avenue workers
50 Gas-pump word

52 Hoopster's stat
54 Valerie Harper sitcom
55 Knocks for a loop
56 Stinks
57 Rugged rock
58 Dynamic start
59 ___ Boyardee
61 Make coffee
62 Baobab or banyan
63 Org.
66 Chaotic scene

17 PYRO TECHNIQUES

by Frank Gordon

ACROSS

1 Workplace-safety grp.
5 Skiffs and sloops
10 Durham institution
14 Picnic spoiler
15 Come next
16 Opera highlight
17 End prior alliances
20 Snooze
21 Wild guesses
22 First lady
23 Ply a needle
25 Rest stop
27 FDR's last VP
30 Cherish unreturned feelings (for)
37 Birds' partners
39 Cad
40 Scant
41 Look at longingly
42 __ with faint praise
44 King or Alda
45 Timbuktu locale
46 De __ (old car)
47 Part of CD-ROM
48 Be pioneering
52 Revolutionary Guevara
53 Dumbo's wing
54 Apply salve
56 Veneration
59 Piano practice
63 Minimal
67 Incite to action

70 Gymnast Korbut
71 Geena or Miles
72 Sugar source
73 Toward sunset
74 Not supine
75 Stevenson character

DOWN

1 Poet's peepers
2 Author Bellow
3 Engage
4 Archer and Rice
5 Actor Gazzara
6 Till compartment
7 Prof.'s aide
8 Oompah instrument
9 Belgrade's region
10 June honoree
11 Importune
12 Ukrainian city
13 Comfort
18 Oil cartel
19 "__ It Romantic?"
24 One in custody
26 Wanderer
27 Teller's brainchild
28 Love Story author
29 "I cannot __ lie"
31 Prepare chestnuts, perhaps
32 Grapevine yield
33 Meddler
34 Surviving trace

35 Collision
36 It follows that
38 ___ the Day (novel by 2 Down)
43 Evening: Fr.
49 Toward sunrise
50 Pinballer's mecca
51 Humdinger
55 Park pew
56 Keep ___ profile (shun the limelight)

57 ___ E. Coyote
58 Breakfast option
60 A long way off
61 Exist
62 Guitarist Clapton
64 "An apple ___ keeps. . ."
65 Dispatch
66 Shoe shaper
68 Fedora or beret
69 NYC setting

18 COUNTRY STARS

· · · · · · · · · · · · · · · · · · ·

by Bill Hendricks

ACROSS

1 Puppeteer Bil
6 Roundup device
10 Patch up
14 Play part
15 Light overhead?
16 Otherwise
17 "Elvira" singers
20 Cloth border
21 Average
22 Jimmies
23 Sennett squad
24 Spice or club
26 "All Tied Up" singer
32 Made pay
33 Theater sign
34 Mode
35 Isolated water
36 Möbius creation
38 Antler branch
39 Emulated Jack Horner
40 Strings member
41 Sorts
42 Original *Dukes of Hazzard* balladeer
46 "__ anywhere for your smile . . ."
47 Charlie's lady
48 Grating noise
51 Gloating
52 Move after swerving
55 "Crossword Puzzle" singer

59 Malefic
60 "And giving __, up . . ."
61 Jack of the late show
62 Director Clair
63 Dangerfield's stock-in-trade
64 Reagan cabinet member

DOWN

1 British resort
2 Feel sore
3 Gossipy tidbit
4 Cruise port
5 Hard rock
6 Word group
7 Fall from the sky
8 Ancient
9 Hound
10 Mideast language
11 *The Time Machine* race
12 "__ sow, so shall . . ."
13 Minus
18 Military topper
19 Orlando-area attraction
23 Footballer's trouble spot
24 1111
25 Go for __ (swim)
26 Rodeo rope
27 Getting the notes right
28 Singer Haggard
29 Southfork surname

30 Explorers' finds
31 Caustic substances
32 Crack
36 Vocalize
37 WWII general
38 Turner of rock
40 Screwdriver need
41 Realm
43 Apt
44 Wandering ones
45 Parser's part

48 Radio-active trucker
49 Great review
50 One of the
   Walton kids
51 Urban woe
52 Rural nickname
53 MacGraw et al.
54 __ club (chorus)
56 Cleaning cloth
57 Get __ for effort
58 *Norma* __

19 THROUGH THE WEEK

by Raymond Hamel

ACROSS

1 Uncover
6 He loves: Lat.
10 Family members
14 Japanese city
15 Racer Yarborough
16 Dummy's perch
17 *Double Indemnity* author
19 Raison d'___
20 Be indebted to
21 *Pretty Poison* star
23 Singing Mama
24 Santa ___, CA
25 Spanish king
26 Rado/Ragni musical
29 Curved letter
31 Start of "Jabberwocky"
33 Whether ___ (in any case)
34 Vintage auto
35 Real things, in metaphysics
38 Macabre kid
42 Oedipus' father
43 Doozy
44 Coup d'___
45 Abbreviated aide
47 Gary Cooper's affirmative
48 City west of Sparks
49 Barley beard
51 Bond rating

53 Cup edges
55 Ballplayer turned evangelist
58 Mode preceder
61 ___ at the Races
62 Disneyland offerings
64 RC competitor
65 Take home
66 French student
67 Dazzles
68 Type of racing
69 Ohio tornado town of '74

DOWN

1 Karate school
2 Middle of Caesar's statement
3 Clue, for one
4 Guitar kin
5 Ziti, e.g.
6 Reached
7 *Serpico* author
8 Italian actress Valli
9 Apartment renter
10 Throw out of whack
11 Major highway
12 "Mr. Television"
13 Ragged
18 They who ruminate
22 Changed course
23 Titan of myth
26 Ginsberg poem

27 Field of expertise
28 Cowsills tune
30 Ready for rinsing
32 Actress Luana
36 Mrs. David Bowie
37 About
39 Blue-book entry
40 Giving way
41 __ Way (Roman road)
46 Sampled
49 Hemp plant

50 *The Merry __* (Léhar work)
52 Icelandic coins
54 Measuring-cup material
56 Strong cleaners
57 Early capital of Japan
58 Yemeni seaport
59 Son of Jacob
60 Drifting on the Sargasso
63 Seine sight

20 HEAVENLY MUSIC

by Shirley Soloway

ACROSS

1 God of thunder
5 Shea player
8 As such
13 Roof overhang
14 Onetime White House pet
15 Bring together
16 Ray Charles song
19 Animal restraints
20 __ Cruces, NM
21 Naval off.
22 "__ the ramparts we watched . . ."
23 Word before surgeon or exam
25 Andy Williams song
30 Taken-back items
34 Category
35 Aachen article
36 State for certain
37 Bismarck's st.
39 Young herring
41 WWII battleground
42 Banish
44 Make a choice
45 Leibman or Perlman
46 Take a shot (at)
47 Temptations song
50 Insult
52 Born
53 Response from space
56 Actress Balin
57 Food extenders
61 Bing Crosby song
64 Sailing ship
65 The simian King
66 Lyricist Harbach
67 __ in the Dark
68 Patch of lawn
69 Loch __

DOWN

1 Hebrew letter
2 Sounds for a comic
3 Gem shape
4 Gymnast Mary Lou
5 Raincoats
6 Certain lodge member
7 Liz or Rod
8 Sources of radio waves
9 Finale
10 Stand up
11 Put into shock
12 Poetic nights
14 Most hairy
17 Sidelong glance
18 Boat propeller
24 __ Than Zero
25 Obeys
26 Of the past
27 Giraffe kin
28 Bigwig, for short
29 Join up
31 __ dish (lab holder)
32 Synthetic fabric

33 Sly or Sharon
36 Harmonizing
38 Keystone group
40 Mil. address
43 Ignite one more time
47 Complainers
48 Oscar __ Renta
49 Wrestling hold
51 Prefix for cycle or corn

53 "__ silly question . . ."
54 Has payments to make
55 Friends and neighbors
57 Is __ of (likes)
58 Suffix for kitchen
59 "Oh, no!"
60 Theater signs
62 Sgt., e.g.
63 Sticky stuff

21 LOOK SHARP

by Ann Seidel

ACROSS

1 Air Force org.
4 Indian chief
9 Fido's four
13 __ Flanders
14 Lucci role
15 Russian range
16 Hidden
18 __ Genesis
 (Nintendo rival)
19 Toast word
20 Horrified
22 City on the Ruhr
23 Sound option
26 Disapprove
31 __-pitch softball
34 Luxury car
35 Joliet discovery
36 Simple machine
38 Bailed out
40 Et __ (and others)
41 Indonesian island
44 Classical prefix
45 Narrowmindedness
49 Mystical knowledge
50 Petunia's suitor
54 League of
 Nations home
57 Don't panic
58 Affirm
59 Computing concept
63 "Hi __, Hi Lo"
64 Turkish official

65 Capital of Yemen
66 Women's magazine
67 Forward-looking dept.
68 Half a fly

DOWN

1 Whiskey mixes
2 Some saxes
3 Storage space
4 Sack out
5 Exodus name
6 It may be up
7 "Oh, Hans!"
8 1962 Hawks film
9 Easy mark
10 Neighborhood
11 Jokers
12 Blind part
13 Sulk
17 Conclusion
21 Sparkler
23 Madonna work
24 Greek letter
25 Asner et al.
27 West is one
28 Pakistan neighbor
29 Bach's a
30 ". . . it's off to
 work __"
31 Tiff
32 Pip
33 Actress Lena
37 Buy at Frederick's

38 __-*disant* (self-styled)
39 Drive
41 Sets in the house
42 Clock numeral
43 Rough drafts: Abbr.
46 Part of SASE
47 You can't tie one on
48 Free
51 Shankar selections
52 Actor Kevin

53 Swimming-pool site
54 Unit of laughter
55 Bringing trouble
56 *Old Curiosity Shop* heroine
57 Explorer or Senator
60 Actress Thurman
61 Buddhism branch
62 *A __ and Two Noughts* (Greenaway film)

22 PIECES OF CAKE

by Stanley B. Whitten

ACROSS

1 Steady look
5 Actress Merrill
9 Does an usher's job
14 Diva's song
15 Coup d'__
16 Arm of the sea
17 Invigorates
18 World Series winners in '86
19 Each
20 Elvis film of '67
23 Actor Mineo
24 Museum material
25 At war
30 "__ Falling Star"
35 Stench
36 Connection line
38 Sand bar
39 Chad of *Life Goes On*
40 Realtor's listings
42 Oklahoma city
43 __ *Irish Rose*
45 Nifty
46 Closely pressed package
47 End a strike
49 Colander
51 Stowe character
53 Branch of math.
54 Jack Nicholson film of '70
62 Man of morals
63 Expressway access
64 Smell __ (suspect trickery)
65 Condition
66 In the past
67 Indisputable
68 Underground duct
69 At hand
70 Canine cry

DOWN

1 Open wide
2 Region
3 Goes quickly
4 Worry-free address
5 Raze
6 List element
7 Hoopster Archibald
8 Completely confused
9 Afternoon naps
10 One of the deadly sins
11 Shake __ (hurry)
12 Mr. T's previous last name
13 Piggery
21 Coolidge's nickname
22 Part of a comet's path
25 Gaucho's weapons
26 Southwestern building material
27 Namely
28 Inert gas
29 Fun's partner

31 Quaid/Barkin film of '87
32 Barbarian of comics
33 __ Selassie
34 Birch family member
37 Gist
41 Big fellow
44 Railroad car
48 New Year's __
50 Three-time boxing champ
52 Moses' brother

54 Give a party for
55 "__ Mommy Kissing Santa Claus"
56 Choose a ticket
57 Showing sense
58 Swimming-class offerer: Abbr.
59 Motley __ (rock group)
60 Jazzman Hines
61 Plan portion
62 Donkey's uncle?

23 WHERE'S HOMER?

by Eileen Lexau

ACROSS

1 Actor Sharif
5 T-men
9 Master, in Swahili
14 Sandwich filler
15 "__ the Light"
    (Hank Williams song)
16 Unbending
17 A party to
18 Film composer Nino
19 "__ *Mio*"
20 Murphy Brown, for one
23 "I agree"
24 Knights' weapons
26 Draft org.
29 Bee Gees' surname
32 Lethargy
35 Post-N lineup
36 First vice president
38 "*Dies __*"
39 Oxymoronic game
43 Asian sea
44 Tea biscuit
45 Rorem or Beatty
46 Light, as fireworks
49 Prod
50 Companion of svcs.
51 Goggle
53 Govt. undercover group
55 Thick sandwich
61 Confusion of voices
64 Mrs. Dithers
65 Urban cruiser

66 Idolize
67 Leave out
68 Army group
69 Peter Rabbit sibling
70 Box office total
71 Sampras of tennis

DOWN

1 Elevator inventor
2 Pasteur portrayer Paul
3 Soon
4 Long-limbed
5 FDR's __ chats
6 Workers' share
    in the co.
7 Computer input
8 Bee group
9 Rodeo ride
10 Climbing shrub
11 In the past
12 Nothing
13 Summer refresher
21 Within the law
22 Consume
25 Growing season
26 Pops
27 Seed
28 Hunkers down
30 String-section
    member
31 Univ. bigshots
33 Rowed
34 Marsh growths

37 Wet mud
40 Desk accessories
41 Flood
42 Of few words
47 Chris of SNL
48 Part of TGIF
52 Disney site
54 Be a brat

56 __ Linda, CA
57 Composer Satie
58 *Citizen* __
59 The way out
60 Baptism, e.g.
61 Dull thud
62 Fuss
63 Jazz type

24 TABLOID CLASSICS

by Dean Niles

ACROSS

1 Vincent van __
5 Suitably
10 Display
14 Skin moisturizer
15 Western resort
16 Cougar
17 Singer Horne
18 Senator Lott
19 Sacred image
20 Ripened
21 Tax-return agcy.
22 Tea type
23 Cry loudly
25 Toward the summit
28 *My Friend* __
30 Pin (down)
31 Flub it
34 Shaping machine
35 Social class
36 Long snake
37 Wimbledon winner in '75
38 Shapes clay
39 Leftovers
40 Adjust a Swatch
41 Diagram a sentence
42 Pointed
43 Prince Charles' title: Abbr.
44 Jason's ship
45 Isabella's mother
46 Magic potion

48 "Don't go!"
49 Scattered seed
51 "__ to Extremes" (Joel tune)
53 Sky saucers, briefly
56 Turkish title
57 Nose-related
59 Maiden
60 Cabinet name
61 Jung rival
62 Prefix meaning "within"
63 Warhol or Rooney
64 Cotton thread
65 Elitist

DOWN

1 Festive affair
2 Yves' rival
3 SOUTHERN BELLE SCORNED!
4 Annoyance
5 Hun head
6 Young salmon
7 A LOST GENERATION EXPOSED!
8 Nol of Cambodia
9 Thus far
10 Sales pitch
11 MAN AND BOY ALONE ON A RAFT!
12 Melville romance
13 Fade away
22 Heap

24 Adlai's opponent
26 __ deux (ballet piece)
27 Box-office smashes
28 Pizazz
29 Concentrated beam
32 Martini & __
33 Given a G or R
35 Welsh breed
38 Engels colleague
39 Calibrates anew
41 Forked over

42 Cable channel
45 *Tristan and* __
47 "Bad, Bad __ Brown"
49 Antitoxins
50 Straw in the wind
52 Part of the Roman Empire
54 Word on a dollar
55 Messy one
57 Super Bowl org.
58 Magnate Onassis

25 *LITHOLOGY*

by Wayne R. Williams

ACROSS

1 Ling-Ling is one
6 Athens market
11 Govt. nutrition watchdog
14 Bay window
15 Makes cuts
16 Grouped merchandise
17 California course
19 Gomez's cousin
20 Singer Sheena
21 *Aladdin* prince
22 Against
23 Mel et al.
25 Pencil substance
27 Shortened wd.
30 Flightless bird
32 Like Coast Guard rescues
33 __ Tomé (African island)
34 Workplace for 11 Down
36 Drummer Gene
38 Apollo vehicle
39 Wed without warning
42 Lights of the '60s
45 Singer Peeples
46 Infuriate
48 Patriotic grp.
49 Copper
50 Partial concurrence
52 Nothing to write home about
54 Lose energy
55 Shirt style
57 Star of *My Favorite Year*
61 Hoodwinked
62 West Virginia senator
64 Sked letters
65 *A Lesson From* __
66 Strip city
67 ZZZ letters
68 Author Hermann
69 Backspace, perhaps

DOWN

1 Bishop of Rome
2 Living space
3 Birds' bills
4 One in the red
5 Apportion
6 PD alert
7 Greek goddess of the earth
8 Some tests
9 Student's performance
10 Blond shade
11 1994 role for Goodman
12 Country singer West
13 Athens' region
18 Input data
22 Shower time
24 Petty
26 "Egads!"
27 Invite

28 Stand in the way
29 Construction project completed in '36
31 Parts of eyes
34 Court prop
35 Peel and Bovary
37 California ballplayer
40 Wrestling success
41 Break fast
43 Nobelist France
44 Indisputable evidence
46 Convent head

47 Take to the air
49 Picnic tote
51 Rio Grande feeder
53 Pitcher Carlton
56 Just gets by, with "out"
58 First name in gymnastics
59 Pastures
60 Highland tongue
62 Bleacher bleat
63 Tongue ending?

26 BIRDLAND

by Bob Lubbers

ACROSS

1 *The Forsyte* __
5 Well-appointed
9 Amiss
13 St. crossers
14 Have __ in one's bonnet
15 Binge
16 Avian designer?
18 Certain newspaper pages
19 Connected to a computer
20 Burstyn or Barkin
22 Corp. abbrs.
25 Skirt
27 Purposely sink
30 Savage
32 Ernest's Oscar role
33 *Les __-Unis*
35 Singing syllable
36 __ vera
37 Heiress Hearst
38 Decree
39 To-do
40 Fills fully
41 Maneuvers through muck
42 Tailed wonders
44 Call again
46 Exploding stars
47 First name in pound cake
48 Flatfish
50 Early Nebraskans
55 Wheel part
57 Stylishly avian?
60 *The Gulf Stream* painter
61 Starting
62 __ *kleine Nachtmusik*
63 Mimicked
64 Bradlee et al.
65 Actor Hale

DOWN

1 Maine waterway
2 Stratford waterway
3 Coll. subject
4 Wine region
5 Rearer
6 Sash
7 "Get it?"
8 Roll-call response
9 Seem
10 Avian trilogy?
11 Muleta color
12 Pro vote
15 Works a puzzle
17 Oneness
21 Pitcher Grove
23 Shoe spike
24 Hunting dogs
26 Make angry
27 Beer joint
28 Bit of avian genetics?

29 American Indian
31 Devours
32 *Julius Caesar* name
34 Lost
37 Outmoded
38 Alice's co-worker
40 Not as fresh
41 Sea World whale
43 Brought forth
45 First prints

49 Swedish auto
51 Zone
52 Frozen pellets
53 First name of
   54 Down
54 *Nana* actress
55 __ Na Na
56 Cereal sound
58 "What's the __?"
59 Heyerdahl's __-*Tiki*

27 CUPFULS

by Lee Weaver

ACROSS

1 Hits head-on
5 Chicago gridders
10 Battle memento
14 Operatic highlight
15 Looked leeringly at
16 Mexican munchie
17 Herbal refresher
19 Frizzy hairdo
20 Menlo Park name
21 Type of deer
22 Symbol of Wales
23 Close by
25 Actress Farrow
26 *Pygmalion* playwright
30 Come out even
31 Coffee go-withs
34 Dad
36 Concoct, with "up"
38 *Burke's* ___
39 Dead end
41 Kettledrums
43 ___ Aviv
44 Turkish title
46 Put in a row
47 Hole edged by stitching
49 Police alert: Abbr.
51 Siouan
52 Soda container
53 Geek
55 Guzzle
57 Just awful
59 Spring holiday

64 Beach resort
65 Hot, spiced claret
67 Cookie favorite
68 Mountain nymph
69 Says more
70 Sea swallow
71 Finds fault
72 Aerie, e.g.

DOWN

1 Ire
2 Like the Mojave
3 Skirt length
4 Speak rudely
5 Hat for 59 Across
6 Omelet need
7 Tailor, at times
8 Film holder
9 Pierre's st.
10 Former Russian leader
11 French brew with milk
12 Ranch unit
13 Chess piece
18 Long time
24 General helpers
25 Mate of 34 Across
26 Malice
27 Comfy-cozy
28 Fall drink
29 New Deal org.
31 Doris or Dennis
32 Dance that takes two

33 Boars, e.g.
35 Quaking tree
37 Troop camp
40 Posed
42 Arafat's org.
45 Political manager
48 Water enclosed by an atoll
50 Engenders
54 Another name for 34 Across

55 Vending-machine opening
56 Send a cable
57 Univ. hotshot
58 Atmosphere
60 Word before dive or song
61 Ocean's motion
62 Calls a halt to
63 Musical silence
66 Drink like a dog

28 ON THE JOB

· · · · · · · · · · · · · · · ·

by Shirley Soloway

ACROSS

1 Long nail
5 Rigging support
9 Signature song
14 Singer Julius La __
15 Wheel holder
16 Furies
17 Culture, with "the"
18 Genuine
19 Point of view
20 Where authors live?
23 Unruffled
24 Social insect
25 Bikini top
28 Midmonth day
31 Cotton fabrics
33 Make changes to
37 Officer's outfit?
39 Ward of *Sisters*
40 "*O Sole __*"
41 Carson's successor
42 Where office
   workers live?
45 Romero of films
46 Jockey Eddie
47 Word form for "gas"
49 On the __ (punctual)
50 Charged particle
52 __-Lorraine
   (French region)
57 Policeman's
   weapon?
60 Valuable violin

63 Church section
64 "__ fair in love . . ."
65 Lose control
66 Preceding nights
67 Brood
68 Uptight
69 Monthly payment
70 Getz of jazz

DOWN

1 Birds' crops
2 Mr. Moto portrayer
3 Up and about
4 Squander
5 Damaged
6 Wood choppers
7 Thick slice
8 "I cannot __ lie"
9 Farm machine
10 Snow or Williams
11 Nog ingredient
12 Tormé or Tillis
13 Direction: Abbr.
21 Writer Bagnold
22 Not fooled by
25 B.B. King specialty
26 Spanish queen
27 Mary of *The Maltese
   Falcon*
29 Ms. Bovary
30 "You __ mouthful!"
32 Capri, e.g.
33 Syrian leader

34 Parisian underground
35 Put in office
36 Grandma
38 Slugger Canseco
43 Aperture
44 Small explosive sound
45 Mil. ranks
48 Most difficult to find
51 SF gridder, for short
53 Con games

54 Apportion
55 *Mea* __
56 He played Clampett and Jones
57 Singer Redding
58 Mountain hideaway
59 Tied up
60 Fitting
61 Daisy __
62 Jillian or Miller

29 PRE-TV

by Arnold Moss

ACROSS

1 Big rig
5 Silent actors
10 Butts into
14 Prayer word
15 ". . . and __ grow on"
16 Will's river
17 Liquor over cracked ice
18 Stagger
19 Heavy reading?
20 '30s radio documentary series
23 Tough to find
24 Speed-trap device
25 Tailless cat
27 Take, as advice
30 Rum cake
31 Biblical prophet
33 Old oath
36 '40s radio mystery
39 Ltd., in Lyons
40 Goes along
41 Dumbo's wings
42 "Cross of Gold" man
43 New England campus
44 Temple's *Captain January* dance partner
47 *Misery* star
49 '30s radio "soap"
55 Part of QED
56 Even though
57 Vincent Lopez's theme
59 Guitar gadget
60 Gymnast Comaneci
61 Cheshire Cat trademark
62 Not now
63 Writer Danielle
64 Sports datum

DOWN

1 American uncle
2 Send out
3 Interlock
4 IRS leader?
5 Grinding tooth
6 Accustom
7 Thermometer liq.
8 Engrave
9 Where Carnaby Street is
10 Wickerwork
11 Steer clear of
12 *Throw __ From the Train*
13 Contemptuous look
21 Nth degree, slangily
22 *The Art of Loving* author
25 Site of Haleakala National Park
26 Baker's pal?
27 Longfellow go-between
28 Relief org.
29 St. Anthony's crosses

30 English channel
31 Hobgoblin
32 Taj Mahal site
33 Colt or filly
34 About
35 Press staffers, for short
37 Mends socks
38 "Set" has nearly 200 of them
42 Muralist Thomas Hart __
43 Go off course
44 Expel

45 Idaho senator of the '30s
46 Physique
47 Whoopi's role in *The Color Purple*
48 "He's __ nowhere man"
50 Makes the last payment on
51 Just one of those things?
52 Pelt
53 __ Collins, CO
54 Director Kazan
58 Opp. of syn.

30   *GOOD BOOKS*

by Randolph Ross

ACROSS

1 Strikebreaker
5 Junction point
9 Rent-___
13 Taboo
14 *M*A*S*H* setting
15 Alaskan port
16 Half the integers
18 Hawaiian baking pits
19 Ken Burns subject
20 Least volatile
22 Folk history
23 '50s and '60s
24 Optimistic
27 Just
28 Honor with insults
29 Bagel alternative
30 "Today I ___ man!"
33 Circle sections
34 "Gee whiz!"
35 Trash boat
36 Albanian coin
37 Gold unit
38 Montana city
39 '63 physics Nobelist
41 Lubitsch and Mach
42 Praise
44 Pillage the refrigerator
45 Mitchell of NBC News
46 Protests
50 Latvian capital
51 Armand Assante film, with *The*

53 Ness' squad
54 Dress carefully
55 Part of QED
56 Kiln
57 Without: Fr.
58 Cub Scout groups

DOWN

1 Elitist
2 Musical postscript
3 Clause connectors
4 Filleted
5 High-minded
6 Pitcher Hershiser
7 ___ *Spiegel*
8 Meteorological adverb
9 Twenty Questions category
10 Improv routines
11 Tickle
12 Takes five
14 Retail giant
17 WWII sub
21 ___-deucey
23 Gave out cards
24 Russian river
25 Little breather?
26 Football officials
27 La Scala's city
29 Dull ones
31 Feminist Lucretia
32 Leaves open-mouthed
34 Erstwhile illuminators

35 Like some tomatoes
37 Patella's place
38 Oven material
40 Like some knights
41 Shirley of *Goldfinger*
42 Key name
43 Soul

44 Goldberg et al.
46 Augury
47 Memo phrase
48 Character actor Richard
49 Heathrow jets
52 Southern constellation

31. ADDRESS BOOK

by Wayne R. Williams

ACROSS

1 Exhausted
6 Small number
9 Dynamite inventor
14 Have a cow
15 Mr. Baba
16 French school
17 '91 NFL first draft pick
19 Loose wrap
20 Western actor Jack
21 Not only that
22 "__ alive!"
23 Less trouble
25 Forgo
27 Appropriates
30 Blow a gasket
33 Just
36 Hot drinks
38 Town near Caen
39 Actress Merkel
40 Quarterback great
41 Big bankroll
42 Quick pace
44 "Render __ Caesar . . ."
45 Softly, in music
47 Scouts, often
49 Name meaning "bearlike"
51 Heads for the wings
53 Commandeer
57 Coe's rival in the mile
59 Part of TAE
62 Stare at
63 Change the machinery
64 Querier re Santa Claus
66 Ransack
67 Columbus Day mo.
68 Most tiny
69 Show contempt
70 Caraway seed holder
71 __ Park, CO

DOWN

1 Rocky debris
2 Funny Poundstone
3 "__ Dream" (*Lohengrin* song)
4 McQueen role
5 Hole starter
6 Camus novel, with *The*
7 Shade sources
8 *The Merry* __
9 Monster's nickname
10 Scale spans
11 Founder of Tuskegee Inst.
12 Model Macpherson
13 Wine sediment
18 For-the-fun-of-it act
24 Erode
26 ADC, e.g.
28 English boys' school
29 Take care of
31 Dash
32 Dull-witted one

33 Book after Naomi
34 Letters on the cross
35 *Cow's Skull* painter
37 *Omnia vincit* ___
40 Barely
43 Material
45 Luau fare
46 Ford role
48 Singer Tex
50 Persian potentate

52 Relish
54 Lace tip
55 In the ballpark
56 Superman's stepparents
57 Bobby and kin
58 Bonanza, perhaps
60 Gossamer
61 Plebiscite
65 Dumbstruck wonder

32 NICE GUYS

by Wayne R. Williams

ACROSS
1 Gilbert of *Roseanne*
5 Title of India
10 Composer Khachaturian
14 Seaweed product
15 Florida city
16 The Eternal City
17 Handy guy
20 *Wheel of Fortune* buy
21 Bounder
22 Ms. Rubinstein
23 Gold measure
25 Heavyweight Willard
27 Explosive sound
30 Social class
35 Word form for "high"
38 Roman emperor
39 Computer operators
40 Ready guy
43 Let up
44 Polish border river
45 Diminutive ending
46 Turning part
47 Successful dieters
49 Pointed arch
51 Movie award
55 At a discount
59 Scout Carson
61 __ Khan III
62 Ordinary guys
66 Brainstorm
67 Divided Asian nation

68 Algonquian language
69 Appear to be
70 Author Joyce Carol __
71 Leered at

DOWN
1 Emcee Pat
2 Capital of Guam
3 Indy driver
4 Biblical boat
5 Seat for several
6 Private sch.
7 Actor Linden
8 Under the weather
9 Spa units
10 Inland sea of Asia
11 Took a cab
12 Closing word
13 Butte kin
18 Word form for "eight"
19 Save from a pickle
24 Like
25 Unknown guy
26 Gets all melodramatic
28 Young man
29 *Lawrence of Arabia* star
31 Determine the amount of
32 Back-to-school mo.
33 Quick step
34 East: Sp.

35 Open a bit
36 Gray wolf
37 The one there
41 Perfumery essence
42 Otto I's realm: Abbr.
48 Author Philip
50 Small lizard
52 Tote
53 Be as one
54 Having spokes

55 Elevator man
56 Junction point
57 Hook's mate
58 Garden dweller
59 Down on one __
   (proposing)
60 Lupino and others
63 Hawaiian tree
64 Fine work
65 Poker card

1	2	3	4		5	6	7	8	9		10	11	12	13
14					15						16			
17				18						19				
20				21						22				
23			24				25	26						
			27		28	29				30	31	32	33	34
35	36	37			38				39				
40			41					42					
43						44				45			
46						47			48				
			49	50					51		52	53	54
55	56	57	58					59	60			61	
62					63	64			65			
66					67				68			
69					70				71			

33 FIVE KINGS

· · · · · · · · · · · · · · · · · · · ·

by Shirley Soloway

ACROSS

1 Skiers' resort
6 Actor Pitt
10 Ring stats
14 Moviemaker Ponti
15 Judge's garb
16 Blood carrier
17 KING
19 Angelic light
20 Foxy
21 Wisk rival
22 Word-twisting reverend
24 Gem holder
26 Make certain
27 Bigoted belief
30 Plumed heron
32 Baldwin of
   The Shadow
33 __ about
   (approximately)
35 Pen name, e.g.
39 Adds color
41 Mine material
42 Tureen utensil
43 Sting operation
44 Quiche need
46 Singer McEntire
47 Long arm?
49 Annoy repeatedly
51 Stick
54 Home of 14 Across
56 Detectives, at times
58 Onassis, familiarly

59 New start?
62 Volcanic flow
63 KING
66 Imitator
67 Gen. Robert __
68 Racket
69 Transmit
70 Decays
71 Monica of tennis

DOWN

1 Sales rep's
   clients: Abbr.
2 Satirist Mort
3 Victim
4 Overhead trains
5 Snoops
6 Boitano of the ice
7 Caviar source
8 Early teachings
9 More profound
10 KING
11 Reeves of *Speed*
12 Fuel carrier
13 Nap loudly
18 TV teaser
23 Ryan or Tatum
24 KING
25 KING
27 Pied Piper's followers
28 "I cannot tell __"
29 Smallest coin
31 Pro golfer Norman

34 Caroler's offering
36 Notion
37 Church vestments
38 Red and Black
40 Steeple top
45 Lamb Chop's mistress
48 *Show Boat* author
50 Foreigners
51 Map collection

52 Window covering
53 Sanctuary
55 Stories
57 Grain warehouse
59 Diamond or Simon
60 Simplicity
61 Individuals
64 Give permission to
65 Pesci or Piscopo

34 JEOPARDY

by Bob Klahn

ACROSS
1 Military council
6 Bushy thicket
11 Feminist's foe: Abbr.
14 Bellowing
15 Diminish
16 "Great idea!"
17 New-business funds
19 White wine aperitif
20 Breaks bread
21 Seafood order
23 "To do" list
26 That guy's
27 Woodwind
28 Morse morsel
29 Inventor Howe
31 Goblet part
32 Get __ (exact revenge)
34 Night bird
35 __ 17 (Holden film)
37 Classic silent film, with *The*
40 Bits of color
41 Come out ahead
42 Splinter group
43 Garment attachments
44 Supermarket chain
46 Doggie doc
47 "Long __ Sally"
48 Practice diligently
49 Full of brambles
51 19th-century Seminole chief

53 Pugilist Max
54 Greek letter
55 *Caddyshack* star
60 Kitty
61 Stratosphere layer
62 Incense
63 Grunter's grounds
64 "The mouse __ the clock"
65 Like clown's clothing

DOWN
1 Mayo holder
2 William Tell's canton
3 Turndowns
4 Spoken for
5 Teen hangout
6 Mortarboards
7 *Shogun* sash
8 Argot
9 Sticks it out
10 Reef wrigglers
11 Song from *Show Boat*
12 Palmist
13 Dissect a sentence
18 Nonplussed
22 Wrecks completely
23 Highly skilled
24 Try
25 Epithet for Rome
26 Equidistant
30 *Sands of __ Jima*
31 Alphabetic trio

33 Carp
35 Boater's hazard
36 Big name in oil
38 Guitarist Paul
39 Brooch
44 Offshoot of AA
45 Ready-to-assemble, for short
47 Baseball card company

48 Tollbooth area
50 Mother in *The Sea Gull*
52 Sniffer's whiff
53 Road Runner's sound
56 Wildebeest
57 Quiche ingredient
58 Competition component
59 Like zinfandel

35 ATTRACTIVE

by Randolph Ross

ACROSS

1 Puccini opus
6 Wall hanging, for short
11 Bit of work
14 Love, in Limoges
15 Actor Flynn
16 Hide-hair connector
17 Attractive, like a kidnapper?
19 IRS employee
20 Where to find MDs and RNs
21 Family member
22 Alberta fruit
24 Birth announcement
26 Heavenly strings
27 __ acid
30 Lettuce arrangement
31 Murray or Hooks
32 GOP meeting
33 100%
34 Egg holder
37 Dub
39 Purplish-red
40 French existentialist
41 Stocking stuffer
42 Ancient Peruvian
43 Sundial numeral
44 Diamond girl
45 Tick off
46 Placard
48 KP activity
50 Mercury models

52 Guinness Book suffix
53 Sen. Shelby's state
56 Verse starter
57 Attractive, like a bride?
60 Cacophony
61 Cream of the crop
62 Rope knot
63 Give in to gravity
64 Coasters
65 Harnesses

DOWN

1 Mexican snack
2 Actor Sharif
3 Drenches
4 Reduce
5 British noble, for short
6 Not requiring ownership
7 NYC subway
8 Camera stand
9 Tea sweetener
10 Gymnast Korbut
11 Attractive, like a sorceress?
12 Gallup rival
13 Understanding
18 Latin power
23 Attractive, like a jeweler?
24 Attractive, like a hostess?
25 __ canto

27 Sleeve cards
28 __ *Lisa*
29 Attractive, like a spy?
31 Jolt
33 British brew
34 Small island
35 Fairy tale start
36 Intimate
38 Angle prefix
39 Vassar and Radcliffe
41 Make a bow
44 Mr. Nielsen

45 Shakespearean eulogist
46 Gulf War weapons
47 Ancient Greek land
48 Shampoo name
49 Peres' home: Abbr.
51 Leaves open-mouthed
53 How the crazed run
54 __ majesté
55 Lemon coolers
58 Inc., in the UK
59 Tic-tac-toe win

36 WHAT'S SO FUNNY?
· · · · · · · · · · · · · · · · · · · ·
by Bob Lubbers

ACROSS
1 Llama kin
7 Morse code word
10 Barge
14 __ mind (remember)
15 "We Shall __"
17 Taste sense
18 Laughing composer?
19 Leave
21 Art form
22 Hersey town
24 Pull strings?
25 Turning tool
28 Govt. agents
30 Pedigree
   issuers: Abbr.
33 Orange-and-black bird
35 Mature
36 Canned fish
37 Rome invader
38 Detest
40 Bouquet
41 Cold capital
42 __ Maria (liqueur)
43 *Three's Company*
   actress
45 Call a bet
46 Reverb
48 "__ Were the Days"
49 TV network
51 Pond growth
53 Hokkaido port
56 Reader's __

59 Laughing craft?
63 Cure again
65 Rise again
66 __ *Last Case*
   (Bentley mystery)
67 Handouts
68 __ Rafael, CA
69 Took to heart

DOWN
1 Msgr.'s supervisor
2 Run ahead
3 Wan
4 Laughing plainsman?
5 Stronghold
6 "It's the end of __"
7 US money
8 Hail, to Caesar
9 Derisive snicker
10 Wood fastener
11 Attorney Roy
12 General Bradley
13 *The Way We* __
16 Fury
20 TV network
23 Laughing tribesman?
24 Bergen dummy
25 Corporate insignias
26 Came up
27 Owner's proof
29 Self
30 Sound
31 Granny's relatives

32 Menu, in Marseilles
34 Eroded
36 Laughing bird?
39 Pen name
44 Bric-a-brac stand
47 Worn
49 Studies hard
50 Microwave
52 Circumference

53 Gumbo green
54 Far East weight
55 Morning, to Winchell
57 Fax, perhaps
58 London gallery
60 Many mos.
61 __ Khan
62 Maynard or Murray
64 Hallucinogenic initials

37 FOUR OF A KIND
by Bob Lubbers

ACROSS

1 Copied
5 Cop a __
9 Arthur of tennis
13 __ to (awaken)
14 Be nomadic
15 Greek letters
16 Garment-care direction
18 As __ (generally)
19 Says
20 Cotton fabric
22 Drome starter
25 Most Egyptians
27 Robert of *The Music Man*
30 Ornamental column
32 Piccolo kin
33 Deli choices
35 Ike's command: Abbr.
36 Hindu god
37 Puts in the post
38 Newspaper notice
39 Horse-players' HQ
40 Comics adoptee
41 Accustom
42 Thawed
44 College life
46 Wait on
47 Dry
48 "Red __ in the Sunset"
50 Spelling and Copland
55 Close on Broadway

57 What error admitters eat
60 Dove's goal
61 List-shortening abbr.
62 Bit of dialogue
63 Area
64 Remove from the galleys
65 Word after fiscal or leap

DOWN

1 Play parts
2 Look sullen
3 Poet Lazarus
4 Entry in red
5 Have ready in advance
6 Mideast airport
7 Musical sense
8 Carter and Vanderbilt
9 Up in the sky
10 Guy with two left feet
11 *2001* computer
12 Linguistic suffix
15 *The Gong Show* host
17 Renter's contract
21 Bligh and Kidd, for short
23 __ *Holiday* (Hepburn film)
24 New York Indians
26 Political humor, often

27 Dishes
28 Early Ford feature
29 LAX datum
31 Repetition
32 As of
34 Author Walker
37 Replica
38 United
40 Western sidekick Andy
41 Perfect
43 Hypnotic state

45 Good for farming
49 Backyard building
51 Depend (on)
52 Mayberry character
53 *Pinta*'s fleet-mate
54 Soothsayer
55 Some MDs
56 Flower garland
58 Plains Indian
59 __ *de mer*
(seasickness)

38 PARK IT

by Lee Weaver

ACROSS

1 *Moonstruck* star
5 Bends in the middle
9 Affirmative votes
13 *Damn Yankees* vamp
14 Ajax competitor
15 Draw with acid
16 Michigan national park
18 Fishline adjunct
19 Lawyer's due
20 Western state
21 Leaned (on)
23 Snarl
25 __ Domingo
27 Take five
29 Little ones
33 Comics conqueror
36 Rascals
38 *Family* actress Thompson
39 Dark, poetically
40 Grown-up
41 Barbershop service
42 Still sleeping
43 Daiquiri need
44 Three-card __ (street scam)
45 Sheet cloth
47 Bridge reach
49 Bright-eyed and bushy-tailed
51 Reply to the Captain
55 Gleason cohort
58 Hawaiian city
60 Schisgal play
61 Not home
62 Oregon national park
65 Lily family member
66 Capp lad
67 Latin love
68 Paradise
69 Wedding-cake feature
70 Word of warning

DOWN

1 *Freud* actor Montgomery
2 Biblical prophet
3 DeGeneres sitcom
4 *Norma* __
5 Popular bean
6 Asian nursemaids
7 Hair dressing
8 Most severe
9 Wyoming national park
10 Needle case
11 Ranch unit
12 Molt
14 Pigeon coops
17 Pencil-box accessory
22 Summer in Lyon
24 Arizona national park
26 Orchard product
28 Not as messy
30 Bring in

31 Brush up copy
32 "Ditto"
33 Jalopy
34 Singer Lane
35 Traveler
37 Corsage flower
40 '60s line dance
44 Munchkin official
46 Pub potable
48 More washed out

50 Macbeth's title
52 Hertz rival
53 Canadian territory
54 Chris of tennis
55 Container
56 Profoundly impressed
57 Uncontrolled anger
59 Roman road
63 Baseball stat
64 Young boy

39 NOUN SENSE

by Wayne R. Williams

ACROSS

1 Threaded pin
6 Very bad
10 Urban renewal site
14 Preminger classic
15 Sugar source
16 Petty of *A League of Their Own*
17 Bet-it-all wager
20 Make one
21 Birdbrain
22 Too big
23 Black goo
24 Cornerstone abbr.
26 Gleason/Hanks film
35 Duck and dodge
36 Catholic calendar
37 Villain of Venice
38 Speck
39 Dock device
40 Stick-to-itiveness
41 Hgt.
42 Actress Lena
43 Clear the stubble
44 Envier's hope
47 Abu Dhabi's grp.
48 One or more
49 Hypothesize
53 Architect Saarinen
55 Corn holder
58 Grodin/Gielgud film of '74
62 Cartoon lightbulb
63 Main dish, often
64 Set sights
65 Far from the flock
66 Pea cases
67 *JFK* director

DOWN

1 Great amount
2 Mammoth, e.g.
3 Thought better about
4 Mess up
5 Buttonholed
6 Yodeling effect
7 Mirror-loving
8 B&B, e.g.
9 Tour segment
10 Mess maker
11 Actor Rob
12 *Trinity* author
13 Where to go for the gold
18 *The Larry Sanders Show* costar
19 Dorothy's dog
23 Engage in pillaging
24 Upshot
25 Highlander
26 Identifies
27 Convex molding
28 Indian carving
29 Hockey player
30 Humorist __ S. Cobb
31 Powerful

40 FOUR WEDDINGS

······················

by Ann Seidel

ACROSS

1 Treat crops
5 Soccer great
9 Rapidly
14 *To Live and Die* __
15 Folk singer Phil
16 Eggs' partner
17 Crackerjacks
18 Castle trench
19 No-holds-barred crusade
20 WEDDING
22 ". . . the lamb was __ go"
23 Show up for
24 Video-game name
26 Corp. exec.
28 Got back for
32 Forward
36 Wash
38 Arizona river
39 Civil-rights figure Parks
40 Ceremonies
41 *The __ Duckling*
42 Salt's word
43 Declare positively
44 Eavesdroppers
45 Seder fish
47 Comedian Louis
49 Bête __ (bugaboo)
51 Raise a design
56 Sinatra in *From Here to Eternity*

59 WEDDING
61 Northern people
62 Mouth-administered
63 Father
64 __ Nast
65 __ time (never)
66 Crucifix
67 Belgian artist
68 Irish dramatist
69 Dennis' *NYPD Blue* role

DOWN

1 Rigg of *The Avengers*
2 Full-length
3 Dozed
4 Discernment
5 Hair goo
6 Green subj.
7 Capital of Tibet
8 Superlative ending
9 Swear off
10 WEDDING
11 Feel sore
12 Winter wear
13 Prefix meaning "within"
21 Foot piece
22 Stashes away
25 Where to get a boilermaker
27 Twist or North
29 Caron musical
30 Fashion mag

31 Calendar squares
32 Talk big
33 Mies van der ___
34 Beginning
35 WEDDING
37 Chomped on
40 Proportion
44 18-wheeler
46 Hang around
48 Canary

50 Mars neighbor
52 Iraqi port
53 Hamburger helper
54 White fish
55 Run-down
56 Jerry's kin
57 Author unknown: Abbr.
58 Revs
60 Turner of the screen
62 NATO cousin

41. TENNIS TIME

by Karen L. Hodge

ACROSS

1 Peter Benchley book
5 Castaways' transportation
10 "*El Condor __*" (Simon tune)
14 Parrot
15 Hair-raising
16 Statesman Abba
17 Wimbledon?
20 Make ready
21 Office wear
22 Open, as sneakers
23 Becker's backhands?
26 Hardy buddy
28 Arafat's grp.
29 Grp. that trains at Quantico
32 Sneaky __ (hooch)
33 You're working on it
35 Baselines?
39 "And the __ not cloudy all day"
40 Candy shape
41 1/6 fl. oz.
42 Coll. at Troy, NY
43 Basic beliefs
46 Tournament director?
48 Mobile home
51 Helps out
52 Shriner's topper
55 Tie score?
59 Little biter
60 "__ Lakes" (Minnesota license-plate phrase)
61 *Madama Butterfly* selection
62 Beanery chow
63 News medium
64 Market order

DOWN

1 Super Bowl III winners
2 Pain in the neck
3 Stimulate
4 Brillo rival
5 Distinction
6 Dish ancestor
7 Gets worried
8 Conway or Allen
9 Visualize
10 Unskilled laborers
11 Just touch
12 Delhi wear
13 Penny, perhaps
18 PC owner
19 Clip
23 Nine: Sp.
24 Pet name
25 Fitzgerald of music
26 Scallions' cousins
27 "Come Take __ In My Airship" (old song)
29 Norway bay
30 Sonny and Cher, in the '60s

31 Clouseau, for instance: Abbr.
32 "Hey, you!"
33 Compass dir.
34 __ over (helped out, in a way)
36 Nation since '48
37 USN off.
38 Leif's pop
43 Ancient Greek garment
44 Frankfurter
45 Simplicity

46 Sandwich fillers
47 Asian capital
48 Shoe dog
49 Sicilian landmark
50 Exam for H.S. jrs.
52 Cost of leaving
53 Early Oscar winner Jannings
54 Enthusiasm
56 Where gloss goes
57 Comparative ending
58 Freon or neon

42 METALLURGY

by Bob Lubbers

ACROSS

1 Greek consonant
6 Terra __
11 Actress Lupino
14 E.T., for one
15 Sky hunter
16 St. Louis gridder
17 Kids' cable channel
19 Bullring cheer
20 *Star Wars* creature
21 Hit the hay
23 Perform
26 Trailways vehicle
28 Part of GE
29 Half of CIV
30 Hat, slangily
32 Bathroom fixture
34 Oakley and Hall
36 Set an example for
38 Fall mos.
39 Judge Lance
40 Russian cooperative
42 Huge
44 SALT, e.g.
45 Santa __, CA
46 Starts a point,
   in tennis
48 Ailing
49 __ breve
51 Transgress
52 Maiden name indicator
53 Enclosed
55 Top-rated
58 Heating fuel
59 Goof-off
65 Lyric poem
66 Galahad's quest
67 Newlywed
68 "You don't __!"
69 Marsh plant
70 Egypt neighbor

DOWN

1 Kal-__ (dog food)
2 Mr. Baba
3 Snapshot
4 Lap dog, for short
5 From the beginning
6 Hatch, as a plan
7 California fort
8 Dead heat
9 Toy-horn blowers
10 Negate
11 Obsolete European
   barrier
12 Spanish surrealist
13 Prayer ender
18 Wolves
22 Hit the hay
23 __ and alack
24 The film world
25 Pop music source
27 Malicious ones
30 D'Urberville lass
31 Music producer Brian
33 Scarab

35 "__ Right With Me"
   (Porter tune)
37 Golf scores
39 __ Got a Secret
41 Talbot or Waggoner
43 Izzy's real name
44 Pavarotti or Domingo
47 Capable of living
50 Hanes rival

53 Courts
54 Verdi opera
56 Penpoints
57 Tan tint
60 Young boy
61 Excavate
62 The Sundance __
63 Author LeShan
64 Stimpy's pal

43 ALL GONE

by Norma Steinberg

ACROSS

1 Tip one's cap
5 *Enemy of the People* playwright
10 Café au __
14 Singer Fitzgerald
15 Cacophony
16 Gymnast Korbut
17 Poetic form
19 Cool it
20 Robbins or Conway
21 Pitcher part
22 Mag bigwigs
24 Appeared
26 Being dragged
27 Like neon
29 __ kind (unique)
33 Barrels into
36 Hope/Crosby locale
38 Ed Norton's workplace
39 __ *a Teenage Werewolf*
40 Witch-hunt town
42 Boat's bottom
43 Orderly thinking
45 *Venus de __*
46 Exxon, formerly
47 Actress Donahue
49 Circus performer
51 Macon breakfast
53 Train-station employee
57 Actress Dietrich
60 Feel poorly
61 Linden of *The Boys Are Back*
62 Jai __
63 Bomb's target
66 Rent
67 Taking advantage of
68 ". . . pretty maids all in __"
69 Look for
70 Rains blows upon
71 Brooches

DOWN

1 Obligations
2 Stan's pal
3 Burning gas
4 *Lady Windermere's __*
5 Huns, e.g.
6 Certain South African
7 Term of respect
8 Ruhr Valley city
9 Must
10 Milland movie, with *The*
11 Kind of sax
12 Composer Stravinsky
13 Bugle call
18 Word after peachy
23 Charged particles
25 Paleontologist's quest
26 *This type*
28 Travel aimlessly
30 Has 1 Down

31 Service charges
32 Woody's son
33 Get one's goat
34 Playing hooky, militarily
35 Early Christmas visitors
37 The Farmer's location
41 Marina units
44 Apple part
48 Register a cash sale
50 Join metals
52 To the point

54 Parisian darling
55 Composer Copland
56 Farm tools
57 Wrestling surfaces
58 Skin lotion ingredient
59 Steakhouse specification
60 Mom's sister
64 Salad dressing ingredient
65 Cook in the microwave

44 IN POSITION
· · · · · · · · · · · · · · · ·

by Dean Niles

ACROSS
1 Sacred cow
5 __ of the Jungle ('50s series)
10 Grad. degree
13 Docile
14 Author Jong
15 Sorrel horse
16 Sheet-music symbol
17 Gives over
18 Part of MIT
19 Clue
20 "__ I Love Her"
21 Thwart
23 Onetime Chevy model
26 In advance
27 __ Doone
30 MCP, e.g.
32 Certain classes
34 Poetic preposition
35 Woodwind
39 Genie's grant
40 Range piece
42 Hawaiian goose
43 "Okey-__"
44 Little one
45 Eastern European village
47 Abominate
50 "That's great!"
51 Cancel
54 Fizz up

56 Beehive, e.g.
58 Apt. offerings
59 Defaces
63 Fuel cartel
64 Three, to Marie
66 Got off
67 Walesa of Poland
68 Cockamamie
69 Indelicate
70 WNW opp.
71 "Smooth Operator" singer et al.
72 Fort __, KY

DOWN
1 Tingle
2 Surrealist
3 Sign of the future
4 Abandoned
5 Summary
6 Stadia
7 Political stance
8 Swell serve
9 Impetuous
10 __ Carlo
11 Polish singer
12 Chipped in
15 Highly accurate
22 NATO cousin
24 Actress West
25 Witt move
27 Salacious
28 Stew

29 Strategy game
31 Righteous wraths
33 Spanish Ms.
36 BBC nickname
37 Aware of
38 Hard to pin down
41 Bit
46 Sweltering
48 Pre-Columbian
49 White fur

51 ___ *in the Head*
 (Sinatra film)
52 Neck backs
53 Brother's daughter
55 Beasts of burden
57 Redding of song
60 Actor Arkin
61 Puerto ___
62 Underworld river
65 Protein synthesizer

45 *POLITICAL NEWS*

· · · · · · · · · · · · · · · · · · · ·

by Wayne R. Williams

ACROSS

1 Starlet's dream
6 Duffer's dream
9 Coptic bishops
14 Sculptor Henry
15 Old-time comic Olsen
16 Pesto, e.g.
17 Frighten
18 Gumshoe
19 Noodles
20 "Ex-Prez Turned Down"
23 Worker's wedge
24 Site of Baylor U.
25 Born
27 Feathery scarf
28 Fairy queen
31 "Ex-Senator Shut Out"
34 Overhead
36 City in France
37 Car for hire
38 Fact fabricators
40 Mets' home
43 Straying
45 Menu lines
46 "Veep Loses Badly"
50 Expected
51 Sphere of power
52 For each
53 "*Un bel dì*," e.g.
55 God: Sp.
57 "Ex-Senator
   Shoulda Won"
62 Increases

64 Mentalist Geller
65 Pope's crown
66 Bungling
67 Pizza order
68 Language quirk
69 Loathsome
70 Signal of distress
71 Swing a thurible

DOWN

1 Middle Eastern nation
2 Singular
   performances
3 Cajole
4 Turn signal
5 Carpet leftover
6 Elixir
7 Game-show name
8 Go back to caucus
9 Small snake
10 Sheep sounds
11 "Prez Needs
   a Vacation"
12 Bettor's quest
13 Swabby
21 Mil. rank category
22 Inert gases
26 Sea flier
28 Welcome site
29 Just like
30 "Senator Pulls No
   Punches"
32 Poetic muse

33 Branch headquarters?
35 Cannon command
38 Light weapon
39 Cliques
41 Flightless bird
42 Chemical suffix
44 What to let 'er do
45 Preposterous
46 __ Austen (second highest mountain)

47 Writer Fallaci
48 Pasteur's foe
49 Misdo
54 Tolerate
56 Cal. abbr.
58 Vivacity
59 Actor Conrad
60 Cupid
61 British title
63 Farm enclosure

46 PRYER ASSISTANCE

by Randolph Ross

ACROSS

1 Nile reptile
4 Carnivore's target
8 Free-for-all
13 Strengthen
15 Poet Teasdale
16 Set of keys
17 __ about (approximately)
18 START OF A QUIP
20 Disney uncle
22 Actor Jacques
23 PART 2 OF QUIP
30 Slalom shape
31 __ tai (cocktail)
32 France of fiction
33 Breathing spaces
35 Woolly ones
36 PART 3 OF QUIP
42 Oil of __
43 Round of fire
44 Stream barrier
48 *Louis ou Charles*
49 Part of Q&A
52 PART 4 OF QUIP
55 Space starter
56 Artless
57 END OF QUIP
63 Words of comprehension
64 Divided
65 Symbol: Var.
66 Offer temporarily
67 Pooh creator
68 Tidings
69 KLM cousin

DOWN

1 Greek malls
2 Tendons
3 TV ads
4 Greek letter
5 WWII fliers
6 Urania's sister
7 Motorcycle maker
8 Type of paper
9 Hellenic H
10 __ Alamos
11 Lodge member
12 Trains above
14 Something to beat
19 "__ o'clock scholar"
21 Dr. Mead's study area
24 DEA agent
25 Wedding-cake feature
26 Wing combiner
27 __ *Won the War*
28 "__ a song go . . ."
29 GI dining room
33 Biological groupings
34 USCG signal
36 Interior
37 Rival of Bjorn
38 After-bath application
39 Hard finish
40 Voting group

41 For the birds
45 1980s Salvadoran leader
46 Cruising
47 King Arthur's advisor
49 Liqueur flavorings
50 Catholic devotion
51 Mighty mounts

53 He discovered the cell
54 Catch in the act
57 Fugitive's flight
58 Prefix for center
59 Kilmer of *The Doors*
60 East ender
61 Present-tense
62 USN rank

47 AT THE MALL

by Shirley Soloway

ACROSS

1 Long narrative
5 Ink stain
9 Lunch fish
13 Russian river
14 Chart over again
16 Apartment, e.g.
17 Nothing
18 Senseless
19 Heavy cord
20 As well
23 Natural-gas ingredient
24 "__ Clear Day . . ."
25 __-la-la
28 Sp. ladies
31 Take from the spool
33 Remark of acceptance
38 Not fooled by
39 Plow manufacturer
40 Get some sun
41 Houston hitter
42 Nautical shout
43 Had a business
  conversation
45 Actress Daryl
47 Touch down
48 "Are you a man
  __ mouse?"
49 Sound from Mary's pet
51 Like chenille
56 Suffers for
  recklessness
59 Jason's vessel
62 Anesthetic
63 Women's magazine
64 Like McCoy, perhaps
65 Songstress Della
66 Dutch cheese
67 Brood
68 Look over
69 Filming locales

DOWN

1 *The World of __ Wong*
2 Don't exist
3 Brooks of country
  music
4 Welcome in Waikiki
5 Venal crime
6 Olin or Horne
7 Actor Sharif
8 Latin dance
9 Rotate
10 Numero __
11 Chill
12 Had dinner
15 Goober
21 Follow
22 Author Fleming
25 "Lords a-leaping" day
26 Active starter
27 Knocked for __
29 "__ girl!"
30 Intends to
32 Betsy or Diana
33 Potato state

34 *The Merry Widow* composer
35 Mrs. Helmsley
36 __ Mawr College
37 "My Way" lyricist
41 Total
43 *Matlock* actress Brynn
44 Came in
46 Legal org.
50 Star-shaped flower

52 Lets go
53 Spanish mark
54 Brilliance
55 Believes
56 Warsaw native
57 You, once
58 "For __ jolly . . ."
59 Supply weapons to
60 Collector's car
61 Separation

48 SPRING TIME

by Bob Lubbers

ACROSS

1 Craze
4 DEA agent
8 Of an extremity
13 George's brother
14 Second name?
16 Too big
17 Do cable work, in a way
19 Hostess Perle
20 Set afire
21 1996 or 2004
23 __ "Fatha" Hines
25 Hoopsters' grp.
26 Swing-era tune
31 Chart
32 Inventor Rubik
33 Pentateuchs
36 Tower town
38 New Deal agcy.
40 Oklahoma Indian
41 Catchphrase
44 "__ corny . . ."
47 Seine spot
48 Like some books
51 Gal of song
52 Cologne, to Kohl
53 Fly low
58 Tiller attachment
62 Foreign
63 Pub hanging
65 Royal headgear
66 The Man of __
(Superman)
67 Edmond O'Brien film
68 Maid of the comics
69 "Smooth Operator"
singer
70 Dolt

DOWN

1 Pacific island group
2 Cut __ (dance)
3 __ Yankees
4 Connors contemporary
5 Tailor, often
6 Inlet
7 Sagan or Reiner
8 __ Beach, FL
9 Mind
10 __-majesté
11 Movie terrier
12 Raise up
15 Dictation pro
18 Berth place
22 Border on
24 Redgrave
or Fontanne
26 Hoosegow
27 __ Downs
28 __ acid (antiseptic)
29 __-Magnon
30 Dine at home
31 GI cops
34 Ship's storage area
35 Get the point
37 Have __ at (try)

39 Out of control
42 Weapons cache
43 Beery or Webster
45 Cut short
46 Capable of liquefaction
49 Clumsy ones
50 Take apart
53 Possesses, old-style
54 Director Kazan

55 Former Mexican president
56 *Pretty Woman* star
57 New England team, for short
59 Art genre
60 Valentine archer
61 Vitamin abbr.
64 Actor Stephen

49 OUCH!

by Randolph Ross

ACROSS

1 __ Romeo
5 1985 Glenn Close film
10 Sloppy spot
13 Discourage
15 Cake covering
16 *Padre*'s *hermano*
17 Not-too-subtle
   persuasion
19 Pipe joint
20 Attendance
21 Up the __ (in trouble)
23 Cobb and Hardin
24 Flightless bird
25 For two
26 Very, very funny
31 One of your contacts
33 Pilot's pace
34 Composer Edouard
35 Director Lubitsch
37 Beliefs
38 Diamond size
40 Division word
41 Physically taxing
44 Miss Trueheart
45 Addams' cousin
46 Southern constellation
49 *Saturday Night Live*
   announcer
51 Ninja, e.g.
53 "How was __ know?"
54 Very tasty
57 Scam

58 Band together
59 Josh
60 GIs' duties
61 Unspoken
62 Cabinet dept.

DOWN

1 Modify
2 Artist/musician Rivers
3 Stews
4 Military insects?
5 Goof
6 Entr'__
7 Clock numeral
8 Tavern
9 Breakfast holders
10 With the most nerve
11 Mah-jongg piece
12 Egg part
14 Middle-schoolers
18 "I've Got the
   Music __ "
22 Performing like Ice-T
25 Pointed weapon
26 Criticized
27 December temp
28 Fleur-de-__
29 Captain of the *Nautilus*
30 Mdse.
31 Lang of Smallville
32 Atomic orbiters
34 Tennis tactic
35 Blows the play

36 Comedienne Charlotte
39 Smirnoff rival
40 Whole
42 Fate
43 "__ boy!"
46 Korean, for one
47 Dentist's order

48 Tick off
49 Play the banjo
50 Over
51 Italian wine area
52 __-ball (arcade game)
55 Actress Claire
56 Film, to *Variety*

50 UNCOMMONWEALTH

by Mary M. Murdoch

ACROSS

1 Swedish rock foursome
5 Loses out to gravity
9 Lobbying grps.
13 Frame of mind
14 Falling sound
15 Wall hanging
16 Contribute communally
17 Distaste, and then some
18 Beyond the limit
19 Parts of Westminster?
22 Casey or Cartwright
23 Org. acid
24 Hobo, for short
27 Line of rotation
30 Available
35 Alternatively called
37 Stadium section
39 Classical theaters
40 Air Canada fleet?
43 Porcine plaint
44 Trousers irritant?
45 Head for the J.P.
46 Delay
48 Frat party
50 Mid.
51 __ Claire, WI
53 Insolence
55 Cardiff art?
62 Either star of *Six Weeks*
63 Met music
64 Wheel holder
66 Under protection
67 __-bitty
68 Ardency
69 Numerical suffix
70 "Touch Me in the Morning" singer
71 Dangerous snakes

DOWN

1 Fuse word
2 Insensitive one
3 Insensitive one
4 Groucho's specialty
5 Exemplar of mystery
6 Word of regret
7 Barbarian
8 Broccoli bit
9 Nudnik
10 Pay to play
11 Mongrels
12 Exercise establishment
15 Korean port
20 Ride
21 Encircle
24 It's a gas
25 Kate's mate
26 King-size
28 Pour __ (exert oneself)
29 Separates
31 Diamond, once
32 Improvised

33 Acted rashly
34 Debussy masterpiece
36 "Diana" singer
38 Dawnward
41 Peace Prize sharer of '78
42 Aqua __ (powerful acid)
47 Avoid expiration
49 Irving Berlin standard
52 Carrier's ex-name

54 Shopping mall
55 Southern bread
56 One way to learn
57 Fe
58 "__ take arms . . ."
59 Things to throw
60 Marks a ballot
61 Open-handed treatment
62 Engr.'s sch.
65 Right-angle shapes

51. THE BOND MARKET

by A.J. Santora

ACROSS

1 Abundance
4 Catch ___ (misstroke)
9 Not together
14 Barbarian
15 Bond player
16 Actress Laurie
17 Authentic works
19 Palindrome center
20 Schlep
21 Scornful one
23 Tarmac area
25 Disconnected
29 Garden bush
32 MTV figure
33 Sweet stuff
36 Fume
37 Bond player
39 Truck
41 Ionian strait
42 Loosey-goosey
44 Fall guys
48 Enlivens
51 Cinematic Hall
52 Bliss
55 Pas ___ (ballet step)
56 Contest, e.g.
59 POWs
61 Oblivion
62 Non-pros
63 New Year in Nha Trang
64 Butterfly
65 Eagle nest
66 ___-Cat (winter vehicle)

DOWN

1 Have a ___ (try)
2 Old World expanse
3 Grieg dancer
4 "___ Blue?"
5 Bilks
6 Horse color
7 Site for van Gogh
8 Hem in
9 For one
10 Bond player
11 Spring mo.
12 Dakota Indian
13 Cycle starter
18 Bond player
22 Italian city
24 Arndt song
26 ". . . beauty is ___ forever"
27 Asian tongue
28 Segar surname
30 Dismal
31 Behold, to Cato
34 Comics caveman
35 Fastener
37 Egyptian port
38 Sundance's girlfriend

39 Uris title word
40 One __ time
43 War-zone area
45 Small arms
46 Actress Brennan
47 Takes care of
49 Of service

50 Philippine island
53 __-fry vegetables
54 Himalayan legend
56 Overhead rails
57 Through
58 Ambulance tech.
60 Whiskey type

52 FOOD PROCESSOR
by Norma Steinberg

ACROSS
1 Police calls, for short
5 Bikini atoll event
10 "Yo! Ship!"
14 Masculine
15 Coupe de __
16 Inlet
17 ORBWINE
19 Sign of foreboding
20 Bachelor's last
   two words
21 Pontiac product
22 Mature married women
24 Garfield, e.g.
26 Stalin's predecessor
27 Western author Bret
29 Opening word?
33 Dear: It.
36 *Pumping* __
38 Zilch
39 "__ and away!"
40 Colorless gas
42 "Do __ others . . ."
43 As-needed helpers
45 Ms. Hepburn,
   familiarly
46 Bus. letter abbr.
47 Kicks out
49 Raises
51 Passé
53 To have and __
57 Satchmo's instrument
60 Genetic building block

61 Born
62 Kennedy matriarch
63 SEAP
66 Think-tank output
67 Smells
68 Sunbathe
69 Heckler
70 Broadway lights
71 British brews

DOWN
1 Scope
2 TV announcer Don
3 Flower
4 Make a blouse
5 Earhart, for one
6 Row of seats
7 Shade tree
8 *Ghostbusters* goo
9 Perot and Richards
10 CRONA
11 __ sapiens
12 Kitchen appliance
13 Compulsions
18 College sports grp.
23 Neckwear
25 TEAM
26 Composer Bernstein
28 Hike
30 Mom's sister
31 Actor Dillon
32 British prep school
33 Adorable

34 Pinnacle
35 Beef cut
37 Memo
41 It often counts
44 Strike
48 Tread
50 Highway
52 Musical form
54 Actor Ryan

55 Renter's paper
56 Office furniture
57 Stumble
58 Went on horseback
59 Employs
60 *Jurassic Park* actress Laura
64 Kanga's son
65 Cops' org.

53 QUADRUPLE U

by Randolph Ross

ACROSS

1 Kramden's co-workers
7 "Hey you!"
11 Wrestling surface
14 Prompt
15 Lotion additive
16 *Exodus* protagonist
17 Former Bay State governor
19 "__ Get By" (1928 song)
20 Road divider
21 Full
23 Hindu honorific
26 Northern herder
28 Playing with a full deck
29 1940 election loser
34 Protects
35 Negative vote
36 Bouncer's order
37 Vacuum tube
42 H.S. organization
44 Of interest to Richter
45 Columnist of the '30s
49 Evening in Roma
50 Horse control
51 Social Register word
52 Does damage to
54 Kind of punch
58 Bar opener
59 *Leaves of Grass* poet
64 Original
65 Petri dish contents
66 Camden Yards player
67 Overhead trains
68 Deuce beater
69 Made sloppy

DOWN

1 Present topper
2 Verse starter
3 Cardinal insignia
4 Tiny lengths
5 Emanate
6 At hand
7 Tropical fruit tree
8 Stay in bed late
9 Note before la
10 Danson and Williams
11 Rum cocktail
12 Francis of *What's My Line?*
13 Spanish squiggle
18 Hayley or Donna
22 Invite
23 Gulp of gin
24 Actor Auberjonois
25 Part of MIT
27 Typewriter roller
30 Pair
31 Blow one's top
32 Missive
33 Melody's words
38 "Sort of" suffix
39 Augury
40 Roy's mate

41 *Vogue* rival
43 Circles of color
44 Strength
45 Slimy sort
46 Quiver fill
47 Fugitive's flight
48 Freezing
49 Polish

53 Ruth's sultanate
55 Shoe man McAn
56 Set up a stereo
57 Inventor Elisha
60 Cabinet dept.
61 Jan. and Dec.
62 Beer relative
63 Buntline or Beatty

54 FACE THE MUSIC

by Dean Niles

ACROSS

1 Acorn : oak :: bulb : __
6 Overhead curve
10 Make puffs?
14 Blazing
15 Actress __ Flynn Boyle
16 Stew
17 Nadir
19 Cathay visitor
20 Question
21 The Isleys, for short
22 What's next
24 __ Sylphides
25 "__, Brute?"
26 Diving birds
30 Example
34 Gads about
35 Heavyweight Max
36 Greek philosopher
37 Largest continent
38 Becomes dim
39 Nothing whatsoever
40 Jr.-year exam
41 Down with, in Dijon
42 Board
43 Suggested
45 Minor mayhem
46 Coal scuttles
47 Tittle
48 Certain Arab
51 Cad
52 Coll. degrees
55 At any time

56 Self-analyze
59 One of a nautical trio
60 Like some tales
61 Part
62 Feed, as pigs
63 Don't go
64 Filled up

DOWN

1 Scarlett's home
2 Sky sights
3 Whup
4 Bug
5 Bamm Bamm's playmate
6 Some voices
7 "Phooey!"
8 __-Magnon
9 Pet rodents
10 Surprise tests
11 Expos manager Felipe
12 Longest river
13 Saw or file
18 Mine extracts
23 And so on: Abbr.
25 Fencing implements
26 Represent, in a way
27 Martini & __
28 Perrier rival
29 Escape blame
30 Mubarak predecessor
31 Joins
32 Sign up

33 Not a soul
35 Raisiny cakes
38 Trend followers
42 Cowardly
44 Forever and a day
45 Pedal extremities
47 __ Roll Morton
48 Hankerings

49 Wicked
50 *Send __ Flowers*
51 Hippy dance
52 Spoiled kid
53 Lot size, often
54 Cast off
57 Breakfast grain
58 "Caught you!"

55 CARDINAL FILMS

by Wayne R. Williams

ACROSS
1 Deli sandwich
4 Madagascar primate
9 Unit of capacitance
14 "__ la la!"
15 __ acids
16 Spring (from)
17 Ava Gardner movie
20 Stout: Fr.
21 All other drivers?
22 Aid in crime
23 Clique
25 Dog classes
28 Poker take
29 European fish
31 __ *vs. Wade*
32 Robert Mitchum movie
37 Abu Dhabi leader
38 Racing world
39 Woodward film,
   with *The*
46 Dander
47 Oenone's husband
48 Ducats
49 Sticky situations
53 Digit on the line
54 Hit the road
55 Gas figure
57 "__ Lisa"
58 Richard Barthelmess
   movie
63 Actress Taylor
64 Paris underground

65 Fruit drink
66 Viper
67 Dough
68 "No way!"

DOWN
1 Surprising word
2 Robin's weapon
3 Bit of legalese
4 Asian nation
5 Cassowary kin
6 O.T. book
7 Do a buckboard chore
8 Cross
9 Tend towards
10 Craggy crest
11 Kitchen helpers
12 Sun Devils sch.
13 Some, on the Somme
18 Littl'un
19 Kind lie
22 Appropriate
23 Line of a letter
24 Capture
26 O'Brien or Quaid movie
27 Put in stitches
29 Weighty reading
30 Word form for
   "different"
33 Cost to participate
34 "Wake Up Little __"
35 God of love
36 Flunk letter

39 McCarver or Allen
40 Otto I's realm: Abbr.
41 Echo
42 Banquet pro
43 Old-school-tie guy
44 Italian Baroque master
45 Devonshire river
50 Rocky debris
51 Clear sky

52 __ Tomé
54 South Korean soldier
56 Unfeeling
57 Ambiance
58 Lobster __ Diavolo
59 Brit. ref.
60 Sault __ Marie, MI
61 __ la la
62 Latin law

ACROSS
1 Pet rocks and pogs
5 Chest muscles
9 Aesopian output
14 Soothing plant
15 Algerian port
16 Actor Leon
17 Lease
18 Painter of Catalan landscapes
19 Certain tides
20 Venezuelan dunkers?
23 Giant giant
24 Seahawks' turf
25 RR depot
28 Part of A&P
29 Dinghy direction
31 *Se __ español*
34 Husky group
37 Irish island group
38 Norwegian freighter?
41 Kick target
42 Swell
43 Loamy deposit
44 Razz maker
46 Letter enc.
47 Flag, e.g.: Abbr.
48 Stuffed pasta
52 Famous Pharaoh
55 Irish insurance?
58 Panama palindrome start

60 Singer Adams
61 Evil Idi
62 Partaken of
63 Oxidize
64 Cast starter
65 Della or Pee Wee
66 Loses moisture, perhaps
67 Mine finds

DOWN
1 Wells' partner
2 Awake
3 Oscar-winner for *Goodbye, Mr. Chips*
4 Horologist Thomas
5 Saddle horn
6 Susan on *All My Children*
7 Jeweler's weight
8 Short shot
9 *Picket __*
10 Zone
11 Unpretentious restaurant
12 Cut off
13 Raised trains
21 Take __ at (try)
22 Memorable mission
26 Part of TWA
27 Freud and Held
28 "__ the Santa Fe Trail"
30 Resort lake

31 Trebek and Sajak
32 "Suddenly __ rang out"
33 Willis/Basinger movie
34 Skater Babilonia
35 Catchall abbr.
36 Devoured
39 McEnroe's ex
40 Aver
45 Polished
46 Icy falls

49 Contenders
50 __ time (eventually)
51 Lyric poet
52 Oven gadget
53 Useful
54 Actress Daly et al.
56 French articles
57 SEATO counterpart
58 __ Lingus
59 Marsh or Clarke

57. *AUTO SUGGESTION*

by Raymond Hamel

ACROSS

1 Withdraw (from)
5 Manitoba Indian
9 Noted chef
14 Wagner role
15 Sham
16 Float in the air
17 Tibetan monk
18 Practicality
20 Car-lot cost
22 Soup warmer
23 One __ time (singly)
24 Batting avg. figure
27 Seal baby
30 Like eyes of fury
32 Commuters' crush time
36 Desert stop
37 Sudden wind
38 Goatlike antelope
40 First name in Solidarity
41 Diarist Nin
43 Car-value reference
45 Holocaust event
47 Blood fluids
48 Compass pt.
49 __ Tse-tung
51 Northern native
56 Minor car mishap
59 Caroline Islands' region
62 Sow one's wild __
63 Dress smartly
64 Soft mineral
65 "Comin' __ the Rye"
66 Hollow stone
67 Mope
68 Movie trailer promise

DOWN

1 From Cardiff
2 Sister of Clio
3 Let on
4 Civil rights org.
5 Fast felines
6 Crowd sound
7 Western Wyatt
8 Left over
9 Home of the *Sun-Times*
10 Sharpen
11 "__ Gotta Be Me"
12 Brown or Paul
13 AMA members
19 __ snag (get stuck)
21 Former Big Apple mayor
24 Promenade
25 Mini-river
26 Hart's former cohost
28 Darrow client of 1924
29 Rolls up a flag
31 Film composer Schifrin
32 Like a multiclause sentence
33 Practice
34 Move about
35 Cad

37 Stare open-mouthed
39 Returnees' phrase
42 "__ to Watch Over Me"
44 Headquarters
46 Jazz flutist Herbie
50 Playwright Clifford
52 Ship-speed measure
53 Sun Valley location

54 Paris subway
55 Bean or Welles
56 Wilma's hubby
57 One of Rebekah's sons
58 Moonscape feature
59 EPA figure
60 Intense anger
61 *Fortune* subject: Abbr.

58 LITERARY SETTING

by Dean Niles

ACROSS

1 Infinitive for Hamlet
5 Runs on at the mouth
10 __ *Timberlane* (Lewis novel)
14 Figurine stone
15 "__ the Riveter"
16 Go __ (contend)
17 Westheimer or Roman
18 Bring toward fruition
19 Pro __ (proportionally)
20 Workplace agcy.
21 A cinch
23 Top-drawer
25 Wanton looks
26 Planetary path
28 Spicy stew
32 *60 Minutes* commentator
34 Rescue
35 40 winks
38 Air dirtier
39 More than enough
41 '50s crooner
42 Acorn source
43 *The Bridge on the River* __
44 Jitters
46 Glass ingredient
48 Lilliputian
49 Gradient
52 Outspoken
54 Informed
58 Jazzman Jackson
61 "__ Love Her"
62 Raison __
63 Actress Adams
64 "Don't dele!"
65 That is: Lat.
66 Painter Magritte
67 __ d'oeuvres
68 Musical sounds
69 Asian oxen

DOWN

1 Bull, in the ring
2 Burden
3 Scrupulously
4 Letting go, in a way
5 Leaf of a flower
6 Pulitzer cartoonist Dick
7 __ spumante
8 Sci. subject
9 Transport
10 Floor cover
11 __ *of Two Cities*
12 Indian lute
13 Hangs around
22 Swing around on an axis
24 Rock suffix
26 Thereabouts
27 *Italia* city
29 Meat garnish
30 "My __ Sal"
31 Kiln

33 Ketch cousin
35 Brainstorm
36 Prayer word
37 Nosegay
40 __ tai (cocktail)
41 Butter plant
43 Ukraine capital
45 Handy abbr.
46 Gymnast's moves
47 Ill-disposed

49 How buckling may begin
50 Slowly, to Solti
51 More mature
53 *Waiting for Lefty* playwright
55 Prepare for publication
56 Try again
57 Submachine gun
59 Hookup
60 Shirts seen in summer

ACROSS
1 "__ Doll"
6 Picnic pests
10 Tiptop
14 Actress Massey
15 Asta's mistress
16 Tennis ace Lendl
17 RED
20 Rainproof cover
21 In its present state
22 Toolbox items
23 Tax mo.
25 How some food
   is ordered
27 BLUE
34 Comedienne Merkel
35 Pale-faced
36 More costly
38 Secluded hollow
40 A, in Bonn
42 *Pinta's* sister ship
43 Western watering hole
46 Short snoozes
49 __ *Hollywood* (Fox film)
50 YELLOW
53 Actress Jurado
54 Whitney or Wallach
55 Lock holder
57 Misplace
60 Simplicity
64 GREEN
67 Felipe or Moises
68 "Walk a Mile __ Shoes"

69 Dodger Pee Wee
70 Julep additive
71 "Got it!"
72 Knight wear

ACROSS
1 Prepare flour
2 Actress Nazimova
3 Guided trip
4 Harness
5 Slangy refusal
6 Companion
   of ifs & buts
7 "__ lay me down . . ."
8 *Valse* __
9 Pulled up a chair
10 Earhart, e.g.
11 Gem shape
12 Henpecks
13 Chemical suffix
18 Merits
19 The __, Holland
24 Singer Zadora
26 Unusual
27 They fizzle
28 *Love Story* star
29 Half a WA city
30 Common title starter
31 Taking off
32 Lion group
33 Madrid mister
37 Slightly improper
39 Prevents access

41 Make a collar
44 Giraffe's relative
45 NCAA rival
47 Primp
48 Pitcher Maglie
51 Hosiery
52 TV watcher
55 Word form for "sun"
56 English waterway

58 "Dream a Little Dream __"
59 __ terrier
61 Attention-getter
62 Mediocre
63 Water holder
64 Beaver's project
65 MIV halved
66 Mouths: Lat.

60 CONSTRUCTION ZONE
· · · · · · · · · · · · · · · · · · · ·
by Bob Lubbers

ACROSS

1 Director Frank
6 Michelangelo work
11 Fam. member
14 Distiller Walker
15 Hoops star Shaquille
16 Compass pt.
17 Contractor's favorite sitcom?
19 Part of USSR
20 End
21 Olympian Zaharias
22 Fuss
24 Contractor's favorite film?
28 Rich cakes
31 Madden's old team
32 Stage salesman
33 Dens
35 Contractor's favorite couple?
40 Foundry material
41 Track shapes
43 Guitar cousin
47 Posts via computer
48 Siding contractor's tests?
51 "Unforgettable" name
52 Actress Suzy
53 Marsh plant
56 Building site
57 Contractor's favorite song?

62 French article
63 Battery terminal
64 Emits light beams
65 Dawn goddess
66 Bennett and Randall
67 Tree houses

DOWN

1 Part of a dance
2 Assist
3 In a perfunctory manner
4 Physics Nobelist
5 So be it
6 French trench warrior
7 Passage to the sea
8 Sea shocker
9 Randy's skating partner
10 Gore and Green
11 Roll topping
12 Weather line
13 Natural throws
18 Openings
21 Physique, for short
22 Part of NATO
23 Destiny
25 Court action
26 Tall tale
27 Sagacity
29 Second X?
30 Cloisonné
33 Chicle source

34 *I __ Camera*
36 Strike out
37 A Gabor sister
38 Overflowing pride
39 Queen of scat
42 Former JFK arrival
43 Heat-loss measurement
44 Geisha garb
45 Weds
46 Fleur-de-__

47 Spanish compass point
49 Sourish
50 Ship's officers
54 Potter's oven
55 *"Dies __"*
57 Hood's heater
58 Important numero
59 __ sequitur
60 Seine
61 Part of a dollar sign

61. MUSICAL NUMBERS

by A.J. Santora

ACROSS

1 Man-mouse link
4 Gets off the fence
8 Conflict
14 Debussy's sea
15 Fine-edged
16 Western dam
17 Justice Fortas
18 Janis Ian tune
20 Singer Ferlin
22 Sign of summer
23 Tobacco ovens
24 Part of SEATO
25 Justify
27 Pictures of health?
29 Baby place of rhyme
33 Office recorder
34 Sandra of *Gidget*
35 New Deal org.
36 Beatles '67 tune
40 __ Haw
41 __ a Fugitive From a Chain Gang
42 Warms up
43 Giving the hook
46 __ Domingo
47 Swallows
49 Fissionable material
52 Jean of *Upstairs, Downstairs*
55 Weaken
56 Work too hard
57 Jimmy Savo tune

60 Easter starter
61 Beer hall
62 Ho do
63 Band job
64 __ Island, NY
65 Alternatively
66 Adorer's poem

DOWN

1 Home of Ak-Sar-Ben Coliseum
2 Picture puzzle
3 "You __" (*Sound of Music* tune)
4 Sanction
5 Ugly mood
6 Electrical units
7 Disdainful look
8 __ Done Him Wrong
9 Second __ (nonpareil)
10 Take turns
11 Currier's partner
12 Tape measures
13 Fish-eating birds
19 Eddy
21 Valentine of TV
25 Last state in the roll call
26 Singer Franklin et al.
28 *Wheel of Fortune* purchase, often
30 "Takes __" (Pearl Bailey tune)
31 Composition

32 Duffer's dream
33 National park?
34 Not at all clear-cut
36 A question of motive
37 Most wise
38 Longing
39 *Attraction* or *Instinct*
preceder
44 Destiny
45 "Psst!" follower

46 City on the Mississippi
48 Fur or fish
50 Egg-shaped
51 Bring together
52 Clever remarks
53 Veterinary school subj.
54 TV actress __ Rose
56 Swing around
58 Dancer Miller
59 Spanish article

62 FESTIVITIES

by Eileen Lexau

ACROSS

1 Assign roles
5 Spanish appetizer
9 Ransacks
14 Regulation
15 Microwave, for one
16 Detach, in a way
17 Valhalla bigwig
18 "*Bei Mir __ Du Schön*"
19 "__ say more?"
20 Oenophile gathering
23 Bottom line
24 GI identification
25 Slangy agreement
27 Gat
31 Fights
34 Delighted mightily
38 Football play
39 Continental currency
40 Dress up
41 B&O et al.
42 Lawyers' burdens
43 Smelting leftover
44 Harvard rival
45 __ hooks (carton admonition)
46 Overdone publicity
47 R-month food
49 Entreat
51 Cowboys' ropes
56 Antipollution agcy.
58 Halloween gathering
62 Retiring Hollywood star
64 Word form for "equal"
65 Luau entertainment
66 Make a change
67 Ayatollah's land
68 Oil cartel
69 Senior member
70 Scheherazade offering
71 Smell awful

DOWN

1 Three may be one
2 TV element
3 Singapore __ (cocktail)
4 Belief
5 Trinidad and __
6 Budget rival
7 Nuisance
8 Not for
9 Fencing ploy
10 Song from *A Chorus Line*
11 New Year's Day gathering
12 Detergent brand
13 Bad temper
21 Not punctual
22 Russian denial
26 Geometry calculations
28 Apply perfume, perhaps
29 Shirley Temple feature
30 Beginning
32 Small songbird

33 Just okay
34 Bundle of laundry
35 Paris airport
36 Hollywood gathering
37 Ardent
42 Nobelist Marie
44 Spinning toy
48 Elegant fur
50 Oak-to-be
52 Detest

53 Brownish gray
54 Lane: Fr.
55 "Cut me some __!"
56 Major Hoople's oath
57 __ Alto, CA
59 Barbecue item
60 O'Hara home
61 Russia's __ Mountains
63 Good grade

63 TIGHT SPOTS

by Ann Seidel

ACROSS

1 Shows approval
6 Water form
11 Medic
14 Automation fixture
15 Scarlett __
16 Three __ match
17 Like some celebs
19 Crowded area, in Britain
20 Tumult
21 *Crying Game* star Stephen
22 Author unknown: Abbr.
23 Suit feature
25 Treeless plain
26 Paycheck remainder
30 Indeed
31 Official seal
32 Bolivian city
34 __ up (gathered)
36 Impose (upon)
38 *Rocky and His Friends* dog
41 Best policy
43 Salad-oil bottle
44 Like the Grand Canyon
46 Mars or Mercury
48 Just __ (little bit)
49 Acts worried
50 Shed tears
52 Wounded
53 Keystone Konstable
54 Act like a baby?
59 Compass pt.
60 Hardly unsullied
62 *Norma* __
63 They're the pits
64 Broadcast
65 Big deer
66 '92 and '96 candidate
67 Weill's wife

DOWN

1 Brag
2 It conquers all
3 Biblical shepherd
4 Sweet wine
5 Author Danielle
6 Soak (up)
7 Walden visitor
8 Artist's aid
9 General location
10 Unhinged
11 Destitute
12 Early tie score
13 Is unable to
18 Medical photo
22 Geometry cousin
24 Name in Israeli politics
25 Redolent shrub
26 __-pitch softball
27 Actor Hunter
28 In trouble
29 Rank above knight
31 Sault __ Marie, Ont.

33 New Mexico Indians
35 *Heidi* author
37 Nov. follower
39 Gov't narcs
40 Acctg. benchmark
42 Missile type
44 Realm of influence
45 Relating to a motive
47 Greek letter

50 One who disguises
51 License plate sticker
53 Patella
55 Nobelist Wiesel
56 In shreds
57 Rocker Lewis
58 Icelandic epic
60 Letters on drug labels
61 Q-U filler

64 GOOD SPORTS

by Bob Lubbers

ACROSS

1 Lodges
5 Table staple
9 Mr. Newhart
12 Tidy
13 Zone
14 Coup d'__
16 NFL battleground
18 Aboveboard
20 From __ Z
21 Newsstand
22 FDR's Interior Secretary
23 Ricky or Willie
25 __ Got a Secret
27 Ret. check distributor
28 __ the Red
29 German count
31 Mix
32 Conscious
35 Boca __, FL
37 Yachting prize
39 Plains tent
40 Prince Valiant's wife
41 Indian wrap
42 Zilch
44 Tough file
48 "So that's it!"
49 Pants-too-long guy
50 Tricky
52 Shangri-la land
54 Sun-dried brick

57 Fifth of CCLX
58 Toll stop
59 Baseball action site
61 Cake inscriber
62 Med. sch. subj.
63 Love god
64 Brunei coin
65 All My __ (Miller play)
66 That lady's

DOWN

1 Bonkers
2 Like "it"
3 City of Italia
4 Jeanne d'Arc, for one
5 Vaccine developer
6 Slangy suffix
7 Ayres and Grade
8 '27 film first
9 Refute
10 Of the ear
11 Catcher's nickname
15 Fits
17 Picture-palace chain
19 Despot
24 Shrimp __
26 Poem part
29 Downhill runner
30 Pie nut
31 Washington portraitist
33 Like Willie Winkie
34 Boxing center
36 Play segment

37 Fitness exercises
38 Pub draw
39 *Bounty* stop
41 Topers
43 Western Indians
45 On fire
46 Wooer
47 Handy grabbers

49 Violin virtuoso Isaac
50 Helps in a crime
51 Agt.
53 Gen. Robert __
55 "The king can __
wrong"
56 Mideast sultanate
60 __-di-dah

65 DUTCH TREAT

by Dean Niles

ACROSS

1 Chess act
5 Remove a no-no
10 Impersonated
14 Russian river
15 Not mainstream
16 Field mouse
17 Word from the Dutch for "pirate"
19 Church recess
20 Sock part
21 Poker contribution
22 Painter Johns
24 Firmly fixed
26 Underdeveloped
27 Travel stops
30 Crow call
33 Really the pits
36 __ at first sight
37 Venetian magistrate
38 Sound of failure
39 Panatela, e.g.
40 Chilled
41 Unimportant
42 Egg cell
43 Earns
44 Night flier
45 Stays abed
47 Cisco Kid vehicle
49 Female warrior
53 Distracts
55 18-wheeler

57 Solemn vow
58 Sprees
59 Word from the Dutch for "tracts"
62 Tooth trauma
63 __ acids
64 Precious
65 Catch a snooze
66 Character in Wagner's *Ring*
67 Noble poem

DOWN

1 Out-of-uniform garb
2 Hunter constellation
3 Personal attendant
4 Actor Wallach
5 Tribute
6 Craving
7 Kitchen extension
8 Before
9 False witness
10 "Stop, matey!"
11 Word from the Dutch for "garbage"
12 Otherwise
13 Moose, for one
18 Trite
23 Response: Abbr.
25 Sidestep
26 Overhaul
28 Dickens hero
29 *Elle* rival

31 *Let Us Now Praise Famous Men* author
32 Says 57 Across
33 Prefix meaning "air"
34 Sigh of relief
35 Word from the Dutch for "leaves"
37 Ross or Spencer
39 Picnic dish
43 Make fun of
45 Sault __ Marie, MI

46 Biblical longhair
48 Selling point
50 Close, in a way
51 "__ a Nightingale"
52 Proboscides
53 Partly open
54 Mugger deterrent
55 Hissy fit
56 Pulitzer-winner Ferber
60 Latin lover's word
61 Hole in one

66 WHO'S ZOO

by Robert H. Wolfe

ACROSS

1 Fernando of filmdom
6 Faux pas
11 Slangy suffix
14 Like a lot
15 Like lettuce
16 Postman's Creed word
17 Gelt
18 Feline monster?
20 Dealt in
22 Lariat loop
23 Premeditate
25 Plumbing problems
28 Pieces of 11?
29 Chem room
30 Sonnets' endings
32 Short time?
33 Pour __ troubled waters
35 Reacts to rudeness
37 Not C.O.D.
40 Apprentice
44 They may be biased
46 Ultimate aim
47 Valueless talk
50 Ointment ingredient
53 "It __" ("Who's there?" response)
54 Uninteresting
56 Scarecrow's stuffing
57 Iron and Stone
58 Gave (out)
60 Low-pressure area

62 Teddy Roosevelt's dog?
65 Got snoopy
68 Linguist's suffix
69 High-interest activity
70 Preposterous
71 Rev.'s remarks
72 Sharon of *Cagney and Lacey*
73 Polk's predecessor

DOWN

1 Sudden flight
2 Bustle
3 Like a bovine feast?
4 "Get Happy" composer
5 Penn name
6 Gantry et al.
7 Corrects twice
8 Uncooked
9 Frequently, in verse
10 Fastballer Nolan
11 Like some dips
12 Not so secure
13 Matt Dillon portrayer
19 Excessively
21 White House initials
23 "Splat!" kin
24 Hideout
26 Throw stones at
27 Have the lead
30 Slow mover
31 NATO member

34 Make a choice
36 Imogene's colleague
38 Gershwin and Levin
39 Bend a fender
41 Like a horse with hay fever?
42 Calm state
43 Yale students
45 Postal workers
47 San Diego baseballers
48 Stimulate

49 Filch
51 Fine and Bird
52 __ Jima
55 Telephonic 3
57 Defeated feeling?
59 Doctor's prescription
61 Army group
63 St. Kitts, e.g.
64 Coming
66 Compass pt.
67 __ *Stern* (German mag)

67. OUT ON A LIMB

by Norma Steinberg

ACROSS

1 With it
5 Comic Martin
10 Bambi, for one
14 Farmer's measurement
15 British royal house
16 Words of understanding
17 Lent event
19 Spiffy
20 They sang "Evil Woman"
21 Printer's buy
22 Wild cats
24 Watering hole
26 Paratrooper's need
27 Janet or Vivien
29 Stephen King's genre
33 Baby's bed
36 Shem's dad
38 Incline
39 Trademark
40 Al and Tipper
42 Largest continent
43 Swears to
45 Discharge a gun
46 Retain
47 Became one
49 Make a speech
51 Move to stimuli
53 Famous TV street
57 WWII battle site
60 Hither and __

61 Kernel holder
62 Entreaty
63 Gardener's digit
66 Charged atoms
67 Coffeehouse order
68 "Stop looking __!"
69 Head: Fr.
70 Heston role
71 Studier of Samoa

DOWN

1 French royal house
2 Florida city
3 Russian noble family
4 Moon-visit vehicle
5 Gorgeous
6 Thick piece
7 Unusual
8 Household pest
9 Audition
10 New York State region
11 ". . . against __ of troubles"
12 Have on
13 Takes home after taxes
18 Father
23 Southwestern Indians
25 Exertion
26 *Ben-Hur* vehicle
28 Make a mistake
30 Popular bloom
31 Sheriff Taylor's son
32 Harvest

33 Oyster kin
34 Wander
35 Composer Stravinsky
37 *Frau*'s husband
41 Experienced
44 Fortuneteller
48 Twist in the wind
50 Bivouac shelter
52 Reef material

54 Severe
55 Female parent
56 Diminished slowly
57 Barbecue part
58 Skin-cream ingredient
59 Gave temporarily
60 Abominable Snowman
64 Collective abbr.
65 Easter-season entrée

68 SPOOKY

by Bob Lubbers

ACROSS

1 Kin of P.D.Q.
5 Small weight
9 Twine fiber
14 Actress Teri
15 Vegas alternative
16 Isle of song
17 Norway's capital
18 Filly food
19 Part of BTUs
20 Secret author
23 Actor Stephen
24 Fits of pique
25 Is of use
27 Squatter
30 Rid
32 Urchin
33 Ancient ascetic
35 Joke response
38 Claims on property
40 All __ up (excited)
41 Stitched
42 Robt. __
43 Sullen
45 Part of "to be"
46 Ridicule
48 __ words (pun)
50 Stashed
52 Marsh and West
53 Summer quaff
54 Blind partner
60 Florida city
62 Press

63 Chess piece
64 Tabernacle group
65 Snout
66 Pot starter
67 Sharpened
68 Mimicked
69 Military meal

DOWN

1 Eager
2 Obi, for one
3 Singer Guthrie
4 Relative of "*Skoal!*"
5 Farmers
6 Raises
7 Not pro
8 Nearly all
9 Winding turn
10 Writer Fleming
11 Kidnap
12 Russian cooperative
13 Bonet and Hartman Black
21 Kilmer poem
22 Roof edge
26 Tennis great Arthur
27 African river
28 Actor Jannings
29 Leadfoot
30 Tractor maker
31 Involved with, as a hobby
34 Wearing pumps

36 Protagonist
37 Arabian gulf
39 On a __-to-know basis
41 Monica of tennis
43 Short skirt
44 Gave rise to
47 Lost-and-found offering
49 Guru's retreat
50 Concoct, as a plan

51 Potato type
52 Elk cousin
55 Ship of 1492
56 Let fall
57 Tops
58 Tiny circles
59 Supplements, with "out"
61 Tart kin

69 NO BIG DEAL

· · · · · · · · · · · · · · · · · ·

by Dean Niles

ACROSS

1 Authority
6 Little terror
10 Fort Peck and Hoover
14 Hit hard
15 Architect Saarinen
16 Fuel cartel
17 Got in shape
18 Singer Barbara Mc__
19 "Look at me!"
20 Like Clark Kent
23 Curly's brother
26 Go by
27 Blood lines
28 Dump
30 Fusses
31 Slow sort
34 S&L device
37 Low joint
38 "Hail!"
39 Skin moisturizer
40 "__ out!" (ump's call)
41 Fictional detective
45 Creamy cheese
46 Literally, "my masters"
47 Operation
50 Diplomatic trait
52 Distinctly unfriendly
53 Like some police
56 Wound up
57 Depose
58 __ à clef
62 Eagle of the sea

63 Killer whale
64 Social stratum
65 The Grateful __
66 "Calico Pie" poet
67 Nodded off

DOWN

1 Retired plane
2 Latin lover's word
3 That place
4 Pipe part
5 Like a tragic Greek king
6 Shows flexibility
7 Paper measures
8 50 Down selection
9 Violent weather
10 They care too much
11 Separate
12 Euripides play
13 A whole bunch
21 Put on cargo
22 High time
23 Like some deer
24 Cat-__-tails
25 Mr. Fudd
29 "To __ their golden
   eyes": Shak.
30 Part of ACLU
32 Mail enc.
33 College climber?
34 Provide an excuse
35 Picker-upper
36 Unkempt

39 Priestly vestment
41 Land of the Shannon
42 Chill out, in a way
43 Roguish
44 __ down (diluted)
45 Prepared the hook
47 *Gorky Park* director
48 Distress signal
49 Creatures of a region

50 Puccini favorite
51 Oil from petals
54 Draw hither
55 Without accompaniment
59 *Les* __ (musical's nickname)
60 Took in
61 Actor Beatty

70 SPOONERISMS

by Shirley Soloway

ACROSS
1 RBI, e.g.
5 Caesar's partner
9 Fall
14 German auto
15 __ *Well That . . .*
16 City of Light, in song
17 Volcanic matter
18 Blind unit
19 Williams of *Happy Days*
20 Witnesses injustice?
23 __ dish (lab container)
24 Japanese sash
25 West of Hollywood
28 Trig functions
31 Donny or Marie
33 Monk's title
36 What the caught fish did?
38 NY university
40 Actress Carrere
41 Perry's creator
42 Opposes fabrication?
47 Moray
48 Character actor Cook
49 Banks or Ford
51 Compass pt.
52 Levin of lit
54 Luther or Stella
57 Rate one's household help?
61 Calms down

64 Softening agent
65 MacDonald's costar
66 Nautical shout
67 Skirt style
68 Latvian capital
69 Small-minded
70 Appear
71 Observed

DOWN
1 Impudence
2 Spring bloom
3 Wise saying
4 *Robin Hood: Men in* __
5 Oleg of design
6 Ceramic pot
7 Talon
8 Jetsons' dog
9 Taxco tongue
10 Ache
11 Tax org.
12 Summer sign
13 Mr. Deighton
21 Former NY paper
22 Mitch Miller's instrument
25 Onetime James Bond portrayer
26 Place for a bracelet
27 Defunct car
29 Songstress James
30 Fence access

32 Miney follower
33 Marching instruments
34 Stirs up
35 Actress Dickinson
37 It's over your head
39 Expressions of pleasure
43 Dry-throated
44 *Two Mules for Sister __*
45 Site of Disneyland
46 Astronaut Sally
50 Rice and Gantry

53 Jefferson's predecessor
55 "__ Was a Lady" (Merman hit)
56 Mountain crest
57 Adventure story
58 Nobelist Wiesel
59 Musical quality
60 Cannon of films
61 Faucet
62 St. crosser
63 Welcoming item

71. *SOUND EFFECTS*

by Randolph Ross

ACROSS
1 Old city
5 Harness race
9 The __ Kid (Western hero)
14 Tied
15 Vacation island
16 Jordan's capital
17 Great work
19 Extra
20 Home of the Braves
21 Other names
23 Let him do it
24 Assure victory
25 Barry Levinson film
27 "Nearer, My God, __"
30 More recently bought
33 Earned
35 Agree (with)
36 AP's erstwhile competitor
37 Pro-shop display
40 Up to, poetically
41 For fear that
43 Wallach and Lilly
44 Overhead
46 Looked impolitely
48 Hebrew month
50 Treating meat
52 Thirty in 1 Across
56 Destructive wind
58 Temporary transportation
59 Byways
60 Sources of loud music
62 *Tante*'s mate
63 Table light
64 Melody
65 Uncovered
66 H H H
67 Ballpark figs.

DOWN
1 Pack groceries again
2 Elliptical
3 __ Park, NJ
4 Fencer's cry
5 Letterman list
6 Punjab prince
7 Discoverer's remark
8 Cylindrically shaped
9 __ *Royale*
10 Has an effect on
11 Broadway successes
12 Worry
13 Wallet fillers
18 Loosen one's belt
22 Soda quantity
24 Yen
26 Czech runner Zatopek
28 Correct copy
29 Sushi serving
30 Not in effect
31 Rapier's relative
32 Uncalled-for commentary

34 He loved Lucy
38 Made over
39 Egyptian amulet
42 Roll along
45 Musically monotonous Johnny
47 Deleted electronically
49 Jazz dances
51 High-minded
53 Link
54 Roman Catholic council site
55 Donkey's uncles?
56 Disney sci-fi film
57 Mrs. Chaplin
58 __ Linda, CA
61 Feedbag morsel

72 IN A HURRY

by Randolph Ross

ACROSS

1 Groucho's brother
6 Sleeve cards?
10 US' Civil War foe
13 __ a kind (unique)
14 Walks heavily
15 Leon Uris' *The* __
16 Good buddies
18 Lawyers' org.
19 Erstwhile interjection
20 Facilitated
21 Heart of the matter
22 Oregon city
24 Sworn promise
27 Log-cabin luxury
32 Visit Nod
35 *Archie* girl
36 "A mouse!"
37 Veep Agnew
39 *Wayne's World* interjection
40 Cause of overtime
43 Bald bird?
45 British dish
48 Ledger entry
49 Like live TV
53 WWII general
56 Folger's rival
58 UN agency
59 Three __ match
60 Mercury
63 Pince-__ (glasses)
64 Bored feeling

65 Sierra __
66 Red Sox great, for short
67 Faxed, perhaps
68 College protest

DOWN

1 Nicholson role
2 Author Nin
3 Bowler's button
4 Poker winnings
5 Propose as a sacrifice
6 Out of the wind
7 One who tacitly approves
8 Teacher's deg.
9 Sound of a slow leak
10 Burn slightly
11 Elephant boy of film
12 Comet competitor
14 Galileo was one
17 Picnic spoiler
21 Oland role
23 Mine find
25 Word form for "soil"
26 Company quorum
28 Like Harvard's walls
29 Triangle sound
30 Environmental sci.
31 Make the grade
32 Adam's third
33 *Star Wars* princess

34 Supplements, with "out"
37 Drenches
38 Shade of blue
41 Norman WWII battle site
42 YMCA cousin
43 Involves
44 Turkish VIP
46 Dips a donut
47 India and invisible
50 Whirl on one foot
51 Nicholas Gage book
52 Charles Van ___ (*Quiz Show* character)
53 Oscar's cousin
54 Draftable status
55 Carmen McRae's specialty
57 Eight, in Ulm
60 TD passers
61 Glob ending
62 Hawaiian souvenir

73 EEK!

by Bob Lubbers

ACROSS
1 Photo finish
5 Pigeonhole
9 Height extender
14 Woody's son
15 Carson's predecessor
16 Kitchen tool
17 Wild tusker
18 Gam or Moreno
19 "What's in __?"
20 Singular method
23 Put to work
24 Star of *The Crying Game*
25 Apr. collector
26 Lariats
29 Hawaiian skirt material
32 Lyricist Gershwin
33 Fall guys
37 Left-handed compliment?
43 Paybacks
44 Fled
45 Actress Bara
47 Persian Gulf port
49 Purple Heart req.
50 Squealer
53 Like Abner
54 Where to buy old knickknacks
61 Start of a challenge
62 Fall guy

63 Shore bird
64 Caravan stop
65 Concerning
66 Actress Foch
67 Singer Lopez
68 Cong. meeting
69 C-__ (cable channel)

DOWN
1 *Jungle Book* star
2 Disney sci-fi film
3 Jai __
4 Rotational force
5 Wild time
6 Café au __
7 Western film
8 Vestige
9 Read a UPC
10 Pop singer Tennille
11 Natives of 47 Across
12 Madagascar primates
13 Ashes and oaks
21 Battleship letters
22 Scottish dish
26 Dolores Del __
27 Globe
28 Chum
30 Inactive: Abbr.
31 "__ was saying . . ."
33 Auto import
34 Afternoon drink
35 Fall mo.
36 Unrefined rock

38 Anger
39 Proof conclusion: Abbr.
40 "Alphabet Song" group
41 Former Mideast alliance: Abbr.
42 *Bambi* character
45 Kindling
46 Wayne film set in Africa
47 Nipped
48 Straightens

49 Belt area
51 Sponsorship
52 Steak choice
53 Guitar relatives
55 Modern Persia
56 Cunard ship, for short
57 Bireme needs
58 Bon mot
59 Arm bone
60 Ardor

74 TWICE-TOLD

by Ann Seidel

ACROSS

1 Young salmon
6 Initials in a proof
9 Kind of finish
14 Vietnam capital
15 Suffix for press
16 "Hi, Don Ho!"
17 *Take Me __* (musical)
18 Feel feverish
19 Covers with frost
20 What a rebuker says
22 "Later!"
23 Holiday in 14 Across
24 Petty officer
25 Kingsmen song
30 Short distance
34 Barbeque garb
35 Go-__ (four-wheeler)
37 Protein synthesis
   letters
38 Transition
39 Hemispheric alliance
40 Leaves out
42 *Uno, due,* __
43 God of *España*
45 Swabbed
46 "Smooth Operator"
   singer
48 Words of comfort
50 Platform at the front
52 Derisive cry
53 Perfect situation
56 "I'll be!"

61 Homeric tome
62 __-relief
63 Chills-inducing
64 Petrol measure
65 Play about Capote
66 Science writer Carl
67 West Yorkshire town
68 Increases
69 Film technique

DOWN

1 Persian ruler
2 Tom or bull
3 __ about (around)
4 Single
5 Made fast
6 Book size
7 Great Lake
8 The first st.
9 *The Bells of St.* __
10 E.T.s
11 __ of the Unknown
   Soldier
12 He and she
13 Leisure
21 Lampreys
22 Afrikaner
24 Prejudice
25 Hangs in
26 *Faust,* e.g.
27 Pressed
28 Chit
29 Proclamation

31 Balderdash
32 Come on stage
33 __ deux (dance for two)
36 Ineffectual
39 Appreciative sounds
41 Speedometer letters
44 "Put __ writing!"
45 One of three squares
47 Artist Hopper
49 Indian monkey

51 Helpers
53 Mental power
54 First name in tennis
55 Marquee word
56 Twist
57 Prosperity
58 Therefore
59 Actor Neeson
60 TV host Jay
62 A/C unit

75 *DUDS*

by Dean Niles

ACROSS

1 Action figure
5 Real hunk?
9 Butler on screen
14 Taj Mahal site
15 __ contendere
16 Above it all
17 Thongs
19 Chicago playwright
20 __ one (long odds)
21 *Northern Exposure* beast
23 Some ammo
24 Tijuana tribute
26 Apportions
28 Belgian surrealist
33 Ballpark fare
36 Flub it
37 Luck of the draw
39 *Pretty Woman* star
40 'supials
42 Singer John
43 Pizazz
44 "Your time __"
45 Offended the nose
47 Inc. equivalent
48 Teacher's protection
50 Lets out
52 "Life is but a __"
54 Lyricist Harburg
55 Wood tool
57 Cover story?
60 Large hooks

64 Bailiwicks
66 Trini Lopez tune
68 Musical Marx
69 Rachins or Rickman
70 Cad
71 Bound by oath
72 Celebrity
73 Speak out

DOWN

1 Nutty
2 Leer at
3 Land of the Shannon
4 *Jurassic Park* denizen
5 NBC staple
6 Weaving machine
7 Purina rival
8 Intimate, as a friend
9 Specialized cell
10 __ carte
11 Courtroom surprises
12 Leopold's co-defendant
13 Terrestrial newts
18 __ acid (B vitamin)
22 With great tranquility
25 Sublime
27 Border
28 Raise reason
29 Came up
30 Detonation point
31 Long story
32 Inscribe
34 Hold forth

35 Inclines
38 Coal product
41 Goad
46 Condescend
49 Use your head
51 Ho-hum feeling
53 Italian city
55 Oohs and __

56 Ring result
58 Composer Bartók
59 Muslim priest
61 Unfettered
62 Sense
63 Act like a bear?
65 Borrower's fig.
67 Indivisible

76 END TO END

by Harvey Estes

ACROSS

1 Angora product
7 Sign of things to come
14 One who decorates
16 Turned aside
17 Circles of light
18 Cash back
19 Hoffman flick
21 MacLeish's "__ Poetica"
22 Chow down
23 Twitches
26 Capp and Capone
27 Common canines
32 Actress Gardner
33 Range infant
35 London landmark
36 Grasp at straws
39 Threat's last words
40 Nut's best part
41 Pedagogues' grp.
42 Steve's singing partner
43 Hula hoop, e.g.
44 Try to find
45 Palooka, for one
46 Long snake
48 The best
56 Putting in the pot
57 Where butts rest
58 Dollars-and-sense subject
59 Like surgeons' instruments
60 Rattled metallically
61 Puts up

DOWN

1 Truck name
2 What noses notice
3 Hour, to Hernando
4 Bouquets
5 Deeply felt
6 Arises on hind legs
7 Windy-day wear
8 In the open
9 "Queen of Country" McEntire
10 Soho streetcar
11 Cigar tip
12 __-do-well
13 NFL stat
15 Bible version: Abbr.
20 How I see me
23 Resort lake
24 Key material
25 Like Batman
26 Carte start
27 Catcher's glove
28 Word of disgust
29 Steakhouse offering
30 Mobile home?
31 Weaselly one
33 "Get off my __!"
34 Mature
35 Good-deed grp.
37 Actor Wallach

38 Beatty of *Homicide*
43 Cheated on a diet?
44 *No Exit* playwright
45 Coppers
46 Moisten in the pan
47 Earthy yellow
48 Roll of postage stamps
49 Barrett of gossip
50 Dash
51 Weasellike animal
52 West end of Vegas?
53 Philosopher Hoffer
54 Soda-fountain treat
55 Potato parts
56 Cpl.'s underling

77 PLACEMENT

by Bob Lubbers

ACROSS

1 Damage
5 Broad-beamed
9 Portends
14 Gen. Robt. __
15 Actor Tamiroff
16 Met production
17 Hideaway
18 Be unsuccessful
19 Stadium levels
20 The Met's locale
23 __ kick (football ploy)
24 Pitcher Hershiser
25 "__ De-Lovely"
27 Changes, as a clock
32 Family car
36 Preschool project
39 Arab sultanate
40 Roger Rabbit et al.
41 Part of the eye
42 Unpleasant conclusion
44 That is: Lat.
45 Arm covering
46 "Of course"
48 Art-school subj.
51 Meal
56 The heartland
59 Furlough
61 Sandwich shop
62 General Bradley
63 Make a change
64 Soon
65 Singer Jerry

66 Give the benediction
67 Fill
68 French summers

DOWN

1 Phone greeting
2 Actor Delon
3 Jockey's straps
4 Polite word,
   in France
5 Money holder
6 Image: Var.
7 Dance club, for short
8 Arab chief
9 "99 __ of beer
   on the wall . . ."
10 Mayberry moppet
11 Bambi, for one
12 Foul up
13 KLM rival
21 Norse god
22 Unhip ones
26 Brogan or pump
28 Poker variety
29 Roof edge
30 Very, in Versailles
31 RBI, e.g.
32 Weeps
33 '20s actor Jannings
34 Engagement
35 Pot starter
37 Long time
38 Griffith or Rooney

40 Tendency
43 Dodgers
44 "It's clear to me now!"
47 Royal fur
49 Alan and Robert
50 Singer __ Marie
52 Demonstrate the truth of

53 Get in one's sights
54 Bathroom device
55 Counterweights
56 Ship's officer
57 Folksinger Burl
58 "Thanks __!"
59 Chem room
60 Pipe angle

78 FOWL PLAY

by Dean Niles

ACROSS

1 Soda-shop orders
6 Café au __
10 Yard divisions
14 "Move it!"
15 Footnote abbr.
16 Give the eye
17 Horn voyager
20 Gave the meaning of
21 Poet Nash
22 Family room
23 Safekeeping
25 Synagogue language
29 Easy thing
33 Potpourris
34 Paint the town
35 Hot tub
36 Woodwind instrument
37 Encumbers
38 Manipulative one
39 Ante destination
40 Type options
41 Verge
42 Popular ballet
44 Isn't colorfast
45 Clear liqueur
46 __ Lanka
47 Inert gas
50 Cackle snidely
54 Futile efforts
58 EPA concern
59 Gorge
60 Giant

61 British title
62 Former political initials
63 Fishhook attachment

DOWN

1 Eds.' concerns
2 Corrosive liquid
3 Folk tales, e.g.
4 Fashion plate
5 Advances
6 Flax cloth
7 All before E
8 Clock numeral
9 6-pointers, for short
10 Beats into shape
11 "Good golly!"
12 Actress Sommer
13 Ninth-grade student
18 Over again
19 Socially inept
23 Whey mate
24 Bible book
25 Barrel parts
26 Poke, in a way
27 Flora and fauna
28 Fish eggs
29 Italian poet
30 Actor Davis
31 Flip
32 Emcee Bert
34 Left-winger
37 Ruth's husband
38 Actress Mary

40 Threw with force
41 Scourges
43 Head
44 ___-a-brac
46 Curl the lip
47 Impressed
48 Costa ___
49 Pilfer

50 Jet-set jets
51 Progress
52 Spanish compass direction
53 Not faked
55 Columbus sch.
56 NATO cousin
57 NBC show since '75

79 WHO J?

by Randolph Ross

ACROSS

1 Rub-__
5 Surf motion
9 Wet weather
13 Garage event
14 Writer Anita
15 Tub spreads
17 B.J. of *M*A*S*H*
19 NY Mets and
   LA Dodgers
20 Scott of *Charles
   in Charge*
21 Writer P.J.
23 Asian desert
26 Pen friends
27 Corporate R.J.
31 TV cop T.J.
35 Rock producer Brian
36 Washington's
   state motto
38 Give marks to
39 James Brown's
   kingdom
41 Food biz H.J.
43 Belgian river
44 __ once (suddenly)
46 Hook's mate
47 Big bird
48 J.J. on *Good Times*
50 Humorist S.J.
53 Nobelist Wiesel
55 Major-__
56 NFLer O.J.

59 Baseball
   honchos: Abbr.
62 On __ (spreeing)
63 The Fresh Prince's DJ
68 Tara's owner
69 Singer Redding
70 Rhyme scheme
71 __'acte
72 Eastern discipline
73 Long skirt

DOWN

1 Olive relative
2 Paint sloppily
3 Radius neighbor
4 Harmless
5 What RNs dispense
6 Marker
7 Period
8 Bar legally
9 Stand-up routine
10 Like magic
11 Fortuneteller
12 Peter of The Monkees
16 Pilot's hdg.
18 M
22 Bowl cheer
24 Ho-hum
25 Runs in neutral
27 Make firewood
   smaller
28 __ *Gay*
29 "__ be sorry!"

30 Economize
32 Deejay Casey
33 Plant swelling
34 Summer TV offering
37 "You're All __
to Get By"
40 Cleveland or Buffalo
42 Nil
45 Communications
satellite
49 Spanish river
51 TV prize

52 Backup
54 Relish
56 __ Paulo
57 Spillane's __ *Jury*
58 Spooky sound
60 First name in
country music
61 Tunisian city
64 From __ Z
65 Half a turn
66 Half a Gabor
67 Freeh's org.

80 POLITICKING

by Shirley Soloway

ACROSS

1 Eastwood film
5 Lettuce choice
9 Edison's middle name
13 Clinging vines
15 Winglike
16 Set (down)
17 African native
18 Betting setting
19 Peruvian Indian
20 When the third party wins?
23 Bro., e.g.
24 Private instructors
25 __ glance
28 Editor
32 __ Noël
34 Center
35 Stan's pal
40 Presidential desserts?
43 Sportscaster Rusty
44 Popular bean
45 Corner sign
46 Reveals oneself
49 Some
50 Religious ram's horn
54 CCLI doubled
56 New Congressional levy?
63 Iron and Stone
64 Survey
65 Understandable
66 Hair line
67 Sinister
68 "I __ Symphony"
69 Historic periods
70 Singer McEntire
71 Low card

DOWN

1 Actress Osterwald
2 Court star Lendl
3 Lemon zest
4 Hold back
5 Farm structure
6 __ Three Lives
7 Bugaboo
8 Any of three 19th-century novelists
9 Roster of the best
10 Star Wars series character
11 Clergyman
12 "All in __ work!"
14 "Great!"
21 Put in office
22 Presumed Innocent author
25 Tailless beasts
26 Printed material
27 Neighborhood
29 Sheer fabric
30 Humorist __ S. Cobb
31 Appears
33 Old French coin

36 Brown of renown
37 "__ Smile Be Your Umbrella"
38 *Blame __ Rio*
39 Notice
41 WWII sub
42 __ Arabia
47 Correct
48 Bit of salt
50 Land or sea follower

51 Comics conqueror
52 Puccini production
53 Clenched hands
55 Small spot of land
57 Be mad about
58 Fast-talking
59 Actress Nazimova
60 Eye drop
61 Swiss river
62 Med. photo

ACROSS
1 Mrs. Simpson
6 Palaver
10 Impart
14 Once more
15 King of Thailand
16 Place
17 T, e.g.
18 They cannot jump
20 Vile rumors
22 Slender cat
23 Accomplishments
25 Eggs
26 French architect
29 Old Peruvian
31 Afternoons: Abbr.
34 Traditional knowledge
35 From Calcutta
37 In the know
38 Hide away
40 Excluding none
41 St. Theresa's birthplace
43 "__ the Walrus"
44 Begrudged
47 __ Bator
48 Compass reading
49 Property right
50 "The Wah Watusi" group
52 Chair part
53 Rub it in
55 Measured out, one way

59 Dose holders
63 They cannot walk backwards
65 Wrathful
66 __ of Wight
67 "__ bigger than a breadbox?"
68 Salamanders
69 Kid stuff
70 Feels poorly
71 Some bends in the road

DOWN
1 Not fem.
2 Turkish title
3 Drizzle
4 They cannot swim
5 Access
6 Wave top
7 Kubrick computer
8 Brother-act surname
9 Pudding type
10 Camel kin
11 __ kleine Nachtmusik
12 Takes home, as wages
13 Actress Eleonora
19 Choice cigar
21 Melting-watch artist
24 Moving furtively
26 Beast of Borden
27 Smidgens
28 Physique

30 Shade of blue
31 Word form meaning "loving"
32 Lombardy city
33 Runs the gamut
36 Church area
39 First name in cosmetics
42 They can't make a sound
45 Lagos' land
46 Gloom's mate

51 Plunder
52 Stadium levels
54 Shoe forms
55 Funny bit
56 El __, TX
57 As recently as
58 __-do (square-dance move)
60 Code contents
61 Leather end
62 Congressional mtg.
64 It's refined

82 PAY UP

by Robert Land

ACROSS

1 Wane
4 Phase
9 Play start
13 Word form for "height"
14 Rice dish
15 Sharp
16 Embassy official
19 Bible bk.
20 Winter hazard
21 Pro __ (hypothetical)
22 Reuners
24 Garr or Hatcher
25 Hes
28 Marsh bird
29 Cut, as a lawn
31 Gauguin's retreat
33 Purse closer
34 French seasons
36 Better than lite
37 Whitsunday
40 Like some breakfast foods
43 Headliner
44 Helps
48 Bandleader Phil
50 List-ending abbr.
51 Concerning
52 __ tai (cocktail)
53 Agitate, with "up"
55 Set
57 Car parker
59 __ Cruces, NM
60 CIA predecessor
61 Awards-show vote counter
65 Bring up
66 Veldt antelope
67 In the sack
68 New Haven campus
69 Dimwits
70 Knox and Ord: Abbr.

DOWN

1 Blue Angels formation
2 Skillful
3 NYC div.
4 Sample
5 Water movement
6 Pie __ mode
7 Faux pas
8 Attempt
9 Actor Tamiroff
10 Tile material
11 Shirt shape
12 Election winners
13 In __ by itself
17 Rummy game
18 Supporters' suffixes
23 Chart maker
24 Woofer partner
26 Greek letter
27 Zilch
30 Giant great and kin

32 Balloon filler
35 Ella's specialty
38 Strand, in a way
39 Groves
40 Resistance unit
41 Drivers' org.
42 __ Pursuit
45 Unsure
46 Dons duds
47 Felt

49 Prepared prunes,
   perhaps
54 Novelist Calvino
56 Hardwood tree
58 Farm parcel
59 Letterman competitor
61 Snoop
62 *Crying Game* actor
63 Little bit
64 Bumpkin

83 TAKE THAT!

by Norma Steinberg

ACROSS

1 Slightly open
5 Large truck
9 Burrows and Vigoda
13 Uris' __ 18
14 Hero
15 Perry's assistant
17 Soothsayer's aid
18 "... in the pot, __ days old"
19 Sammy or Geena
20 Unlawful payments
22 Arrests
23 Ceremony
24 Brave
25 Leaf
28 Angelic higher-up
30 "Bye!"
32 Absorb
33 Mme. Bovary
37 Swiveled
39 Summer fruit
41 Strong __ ox
42 Ensnare
44 Scarcity
45 Kind of piano
48 Gibbons
49 Use the tub
51 Potpourri: Abbr.
53 __ firma
54 Libation container
59 "To __ human"
60 West Point monogram

61 Gumbo ingredient
62 *Golden Hind* captain
63 Authentic
64 Mortgage, e.g.
65 Yes votes
66 Writer Ferber
67 Be inclined

DOWN

1 Frenzied
2 Guitarist Hendrix
3 William Baldwin's brother
4 Standing
5 Egyptian peninsula
6 Decrees
7 Tork, Nesmith et al.
8 Islands, to Pierre
9 Makes sense
10 Get off
11 Santa's helpers
12 Yucky
16 Burro
21 *Dark Victory* costar
24 Stared slack-jawed
25 French veggie choice
26 Menlo Park middle name
27 Walk out
29 Carl Reiner's son
30 Fitness center
31 *Aladdin* character
34 Swamp

35 Series winners in '69
36 Baseball-bat wood
38 Aykroyd or Quayle
40 Stretch (for)
43 Puzzled
46 Stages of development
47 Jack Haley part
49 Oft-quoted catcher

50 Display
52 La __ (opera house)
53 Danson or Knight
54 Immaculate
55 Dash off
56 Tom Joad, e.g.
57 Small brown bird
58 Come to earth

84 GONG SHOW

by Ann Seidel

ACROSS

1 Revolver guy
5 Street actor
9 Vaccine discoverer
14 Capital of Samoa
15 Love, to Luis
16 __ France
17 Kook
19 Thousand, in France
20 Compass pt.
21 Lean
22 More exalted
23 Wound up
25 Like some endings
27 __, *the Beloved Country*
28 Like some losers
29 City on the Danube
32 Fancy tie
35 Chew the fat
36 Runny cheese
37 Name of two presidents
39 Puts away
41 "I cannot tell __"
42 Media mogul Zuckerman
44 Calls for
45 CD-__ (computer-disk type)
46 Fill to excess
47 __ mot (witticism)
48 Prickled

50 Meadows or Hepburn
54 Biological subdivisions
56 Viet __
58 Kimono sash
59 Seaweed
60 Chocolate-chip cookie
62 "*Für __*"
63 Villain in *Othello*
64 Darmstadt donkey
65 Country roads
66 Bandleader Kenton
67 Tear apart

DOWN

1 Military-school student
2 Give one's views
3 Bedding
4 Kid's game
5 What ails you
6 "__ the Mood for Love"
7 Solitary
8 Work unit
9 Cinema's Signoret
10 Excuse
11 Graphic distribution
12 Unemployed
13 __-do-well
18 Puts on notice
22 1994 Rob Reiner film
24 Tea biscuit
26 Cook beef
30 Fibbed
31 Army meal

32 Open a bit
33 Go it alone
34 Speaking up
35 Big bill
36 Intermingle
38 Missouri River city
40 Adequate
43 1776 soldier
46 Masses of loose rock
47 Knit-shirt material

49 Needle
51 Get out of bed
52 TV's Jed Clampett
53 Bond return
54 Highlander
55 Scat name
57 Gymnast Korbut
60 "__ the season
   to be jolly"
61 On top of, poetically

85 CLOSE CALLS

by Dean Niles

ACROSS
1 Bettor's tactic
6 Seniors grp.
10 Surfer's surface
14 Eskimo relative
15 Blackjack prop
16 Tel __
17 Tithing portion
18 CLOSE
20 "__ Jude"
21 Tabloid twosomes
23 Ponders
24 English racing venue
26 Grunts
27 Disqualify, in court
29 German capitalist?
34 Letter openers
35 Reporter Bly
37 Comic Philips
38 Beats it
39 Mr. T's group
40 "Just the facts, __"
41 Loop conveyances
42 Foreboding aura
43 Joliet discovery
44 Extracts, in a way
46 Waterways
48 Possesses
49 Tycoon from Texarkana
50 Vapor
53 Swarming throng
55 Hawaiian Punch rival
58 CLOSE

60 Under, to a poet
62 Spiny plant
63 Saturn or Mercury
64 *Inferno* poet
65 Porgy's love
66 Fall rudely
67 "Bloody Mary" was one

DOWN
1 "Hell __ no fury . . ."
2 Robt. __
3 CLOSE
4 Stomach
5 B-school topic
6 Black-ink item
7 "Might I interrupt?"
8 Mythical birds
9 For each
10 '60s dance
11 Budget competitor
12 Long live: Fr.
13 12/24 and 12/31
19 Rousseau work
22 Pedicurist's concern
25 Beer
26 Smirked
27 Displayed ire
28 Italian town
29 Consecrate
30 Veteran actor Jack
31 CLOSE
32 Internet missive

33 Some apples
36 Footnote phrase
40 Less, in music
42 Where US 95 ends
45 London river
47 "Banality of evil" philosopher
49 Hospital area, for short
50 Pierce

51 The T in TV
52 Love god
53 Truckers do it
54 __ von Bismarck
56 "Take __ the Limit" (Eagles tune)
57 *Mask* star
59 40 winks
61 __ *de vie* (brandy)

86 THE SOUND OF MUSIC

by Bob Lubbers

ACROSS

1 Pol.'s money source
4 Tendon
9 Senegal capital
14 He played Tarzan
15 Doe follower
16 Portrait
17 Shade tree
18 Couch potato's complaint?
20 Shul teacher
22 Cul de __
23 Stone or Gless
25 Steady currents
29 Singer Julius
31 Originate
33 __-relief
35 Prepare to take off
37 Bayes and Ephron
38 Sacro ending
41 GI address
42 Stumbling blocks
43 Small band
44 Repetition method
46 Bee follower
47 "I __ Care"
49 Battleground of 1943
52 Reel men?
54 Southwestern bricks
57 Santa __, CA
58 *Lorna* __
59 Dessert?
66 Western Indian
67 Eaglets' nursery
68 Drew or DeGeneres
69 Actor Beatty
70 Mix
71 Doesn't walk
72 Towel (off)

DOWN

1 Equals
2 Islam's Almighty
3 Pieman's customer?
4 Rescuer
5 General Amin
6 Classic beginning
7 Slithery swimmer
8 Watch place
9 Detects
10 Latin 101 word
11 Auntie Em's st.
12 T-man, e.g.
13 Run up an engine
19 DEA man
21 Bikini part
24 Like it or __
25 Star personas?
26 Uncountable years
27 Leather-covered?
28 __ *Door Canteen*
30 German river
32 Latin being
33 Pen names
34 Kauai "Bye!"
36 Bit

39 Snug as __ ...
40 Nabbed
45 Memorable period
48 Declare false
50 Accessories
51 Court
53 It's built for speed
55 Enrol

56 Squalid
59 Bandleader Calloway
60 Norse goddess
61 Before, poetically
62 __-Tin-Tin
63 Yalie
64 Lawyer's deg.
65 Peggy or Pinky

87. ????
by Norma Steinberg

ACROSS
1 Sound of a guffaw
5 Shore spot
10 In __ (lined up)
14 Composer Stravinsky
15 Cornered
16 Jacob's first wife
17 Speaker Gingrich
18 Heat unit
19 Ricki or Veronica
20 Conclusion
21 Question from Lou Costello
23 Tales
25 Hive resident
26 Three feet
27 Theater street
32 Mick Jagger, e.g.
34 Elevator stop
35 Hurry
36 *The Winds of War* author
37 Invigorating
38 Baby's first word, perhaps
39 Annex
40 VCR button
41 Irrigate
42 Marina slots
44 Earth's neighbor
45 Actress MacGraw
46 Truthful
49 Kids' picture-game book

54 In favor of
55 Leave the path
56 Hang around
57 Bloodhound's clue
58 Genesis son
59 Writer Jong
60 Capitol topper
61 Small horse
62 Office furniture
63 Read, as a bar code

DOWN
1 Dancer Gregory
2 Representative
3 Words upon meeting
4 "Wherefore __ thou?"
5 Soaked
6 Group's personality
7 Burrows and Vigoda
8 Dear: It.
9 Churchgoer's carry-along
10 Connected by treaty
11 Hindmost part
12 Grown acorns
13 Sharpen
21 Current conduit
22 Phobia
24 Hierarchical standing
27 Ecstasy
28 Kennedy matriarch
29 Mel Blanc line

30 Adjutant
31 Part of a decade
32 Did the crawl
33 Brouhaha
34 Kin of the twist
37 Sent into exile
38 Pub missile
40 Heap
41 Texas town
43 Once in a blue moon

44 Cotton cloth
46 Speckle
47 Bouquet
48 *Two Women* star
49 Prepare presents
50 King of the road
51 Not odd
52 Had on
53 Hertz rival
57 "__ bodkins!"

88 TV LAWMEN

by Rich Norris

ACROSS

1 Shopper's burden
5 Spiny-leaved plant
10 Touch on
14 Scandinavian capital
15 __ fours (French cookies)
16 Create
17 '60s TV cops
20 Salon rinse
21 Most small and round, as eyes
22 Turns down the light
25 In no way
26 Clairvoyance, for short
29 Let down
32 Birdman of Alcatraz, e.g.
36 Leak out slowly
38 Showed up
39 French verse
40 '70s TV cops
43 Artist's need
44 Rigatoni relative
45 "__ pin, pick it up . . ."
46 Allen or Martin
47 Choose democratically
49 Society girl, for short
50 NRC's ancestor
52 Classic cars
54 Think over
59 Island south of Sicily
63 '80s TV cops

66 Away from the wind
67 Powerfully built
68 Drive the getaway car
69 Used 20 Across
70 Agreements
71 *Ghost* star Moore

DOWN

1 This and that?
2 Arthur of tennis
3 Valley
4 Like a good argument
5 Suitable
6 Metro or Prizm
7 ". . . three men in __"
8 __ versa
9 Patriot Allen
10 Upwardly mobile
11 Hay unit
12 Luau strings, briefly
13 Student's concern
18 Use a hammer
19 Lyricist Green
23 Poke fun at
24 *Ghost* star Patrick
26 Sharp curves
27 Attack
28 "__ porridge hot . . ."
30 PC communication
31 Lessee
33 Gave a banquet for
34 Quiz host
35 Detox, perhaps

37 Came out on top
41 Frozen rainfalls
42 Vegas cubes
48 Pyramid, essentially
51 Cartoonist Guisewhite
53 Dinner course
54 Country south of Libya
55 Slick

56 Jocularity
57 Quiz answer
58 Congers
60 Garage job
61 Pour
62 Italian wine region
64 __ out a living
65 Cobb and Hardin

89 CROSS-SWORD PUZZLE

by Dean Niles

ACROSS

1 Before deductions
6 "Get __ of that!"
11 Cold War org.
14 Part of USNA
15 Worth
16 That girl
17 Caribbean resort
18 Put an __ (terminate)
19 Santa __, CA
20 Liquefy again
22 Powdery residue
23 Comic scene
24 Former Virginia senator
26 Dice-game bugs
28 Like some undershirts
31 Goad
32 Israeli dance
33 Transfixed
35 Prier's need
39 Discharges
41 Pa. neighbor
42 Marry on the run
43 March, e.g.
44 Historic times
46 Exultation
47 TV producer Norman
49 Went off, in a way
51 Former Romanian president
54 Freight hauler
55 Aggregation
56 Sturm __ Drang
58 Disconnect
62 "Peggy __" (Holly tune)
63 Parking penalties
65 Textile fiber
66 Goof up
67 Particulars
68 Slow gaits
69 Rebel Turner
70 English poet
71 Donkeys

DOWN

1 Growl
2 Out of the ordinary
3 Egg cell
4 Flexed one's muscles
5 Zigzag course
6 "__ Maria"
7 Singer Cantrell
8 Midsize car
9 Poet or playwright
10 __ volente (God willing)
11 Coarse fabric
12 Bottle occupant
13 Little terrors
21 Ski lift
23 Uke kin
25 Harrison Ford film
27 Give the eye
28 '54 sci-fi film
29 __ sapiens
30 Land of the Shannon

34 For each
36 Electrical unit
37 Fencer's arm
38 Grass stalk
40 "__ Always a Woman"
45 Tore off
48 Keenness
50 Oath of silence
51 *Peer Gynt* playwright

52 Actress Dern
53 Like some gases
57 Spec recording
59 Singer Tori
60 Summon to court
61 Dame Myra
63 Fish story
64 123-45-6789,
e.g.: Abbr.

90 BEASTLY

by Bob Lubbers

ACROSS

1 "__ the ramparts . . ."
4 Does sum work
8 Hide
13 John and Maureen's daughter
14 Go bad
15 Squander
16 Missile path, e.g.
17 Uproar over a bear?
19 Start a Model T again
21 Classic start
22 Innie opposite
23 Alphonse's partner
27 EPA concern
29 Engine pt.
31 "You're __" (Porter tune)
33 Brinker or Conried
34 Dumbarton __
36 Words from Caesar
37 Some MDs' specialties
38 Poetic conjunction
39 Pitch detector
40 Per-__ worker
42 Greek goddess
43 Part of A&E
44 Grads
46 Hearst's captors
48 Swiss abstractionist
49 Secret
51 Intermission follower

53 Paths: Abbr.
54 Pruned
57 Musical king?
62 Ore. neighbor
63 Sink unclogger
64 Discharge
65 Allen of *Home Improvement*
66 Muscle
67 Nitti nemesis
68 Understand

DOWN

1 Ike contemporary
2 The Auld Sod
3 Masked storyteller?
4 "It's __!" ("Very funny!")
5 Burdened idealist?
6 Carried out
7 Street talk
8 Sound of speed
9 Treat hide
10 __ *Lay Dying*
11 R-V connectors
12 Dress end
14 Mini-feud
18 Deli slices
20 Runners, e.g.
24 Driver's peg
25 Mammal boundaries?
26 Jot
27 "I did not think to __ tear": Shak.

28 Envelope material
30 John and Bert
32 Prize money
35 Cuddly one's traits?
41 End of this century
42 Vedas reader
43 Actor Tamiroff
45 Straight's partner
47 Not like this clue

50 German city
52 Apply color
55 Sedgwick or Brickell
56 May Whitty, e.g.
57 TV spots
58 Dernier __
59 Role for Harrison
60 Single
61 Bigger than med.

91. NUMEROUS THINGS

by Harvey Estes

ACROSS

1 Save companion
7 Least risky
13 Mined find
15 Recover from
16 Delivery room worker?
17 Reporter's fix-up
18 Card game
20 Book of legends?
21 Poet's product
22 Hear a case
23 __ up (make sense)
26 Fidgety
28 Bay baby, maybe
32 Some combos
34 Taco need
36 *The __ Bears*
39 Fans of the cotton bole?
40 He can't remember
42 Denim pants
43 Poet Allen
44 General Patton
47 Workplace-fairness abbr.
48 Tag pursuers
50 Mauna __
51 Fairway border
54 Girls' mag
60 They take a bow
62 Like a rubber band
63 Israel-Jordan divider
64 He did it his way
65 __ out (exhausted)
66 Lifework

DOWN

1 Riverbank deposit
2 Where it may stick
3 Pajama coverer
4 Privy to
5 Comedian Sahl
6 Victimize
7 Exercize the eyes
8 Engaged in hostilities
9 Two-tune record
10 Eye opener?
11 __ good example
12 Very, in Verdun
14 Eat at
15 Coll. sr.'s test
19 Unmixed
22 Phoenician city
23 Near home?
24 O'Neill work
25 "I __ Get to Sleep at All"
26 Purposes
27 Miss Piggy, for one
29 Popeye's goyl
30 *Kate & __*
31 Capture in a loop
33 U-turn
35 Phone front
37 Spare hair
38 Unstamped enc.

41 Merry king
45 Wanders
46 Highlanders' language
49 Objects nearby
51 Grating sound
52 Reverend Roberts
53 '95 NCAA champ

54 FICA funds it
55 Singer Mouskouri
56 Pre-revolution ruler
57 Kitchen extension
58 Land of Yeats
59 Former CSA state
61 Football great Grange

92

HOLD IT
· ·
by Shirley Soloway

ACROSS
1 Tree fluids
5 Tartan design
10 Sore feeling
14 Busy as __
15 Mexican rope
16 New York stadium
17 Go to bed
19 Get wind of
20 Baking potatoes
21 Truthful
23 Barbara __ Geddes
24 Musical notes
26 Add color to
27 Sure to happen
30 Reno's st.
33 Claims
36 Cache box?
37 Get away from
39 __ Gay (WWII plane)
41 Hacienda Mrs.
42 "__ Be Me"
43 Of an insect part
44 Care for
46 Regarding
47 Hosp. areas
48 Whodunit devices
51 Grass-animal name
53 Genetic initials
54 747, e.g.
57 Most flirty
59 Recessed area
61 Challenge

62 Social service
   employer
65 Pizza cooker
66 Japanese dog
67 Poetic dusks
68 Western plateau
69 Artist Neiman
70 33 Down artist

DOWN
1 Indian term
   of address
2 Tolerate
3 Posy part
4 Son of Adam
5 Adjusts ahead of time
6 Fleur-de-__
7 Motorists' org.
8 Annoying sensation
9 Former U.S. territory
10 Pale-faced
11 Stale jokes
12 Summer discomfort
13 Pitcher part
18 Brass instrument
22 Actor Bruce
   or Hawthorne
25 Daisy type
27 Cuba, e.g.: Sp.
28 Actor Zimbalist
29 Socked on the head
31 Revise
32 Turn down

33 Art ___
34 "Are you ___ out?"
35 Sports stats
38 Grazing grounds
40 Michael Caine role
45 Actress Faye
49 Mischief-maker
50 ___ Alto, CA
52 Laughing mammal

54 Batman's nemesis
55 Occasion
56 Short and sweet
57 Hideaway
58 Accept
60 Northern native
61 Funnyman DeLuise
63 Knightly title
64 WWII region

93 PARTY TIME
by Mary Brindamour

ACROSS
1 Vessel for wine
5 Music symbols
10 During
14 Hurt
15 Springfield or carbine
16 Space grp.
17 Persia, today
18 Deli patron
19 Prof.'s helper
20 Party time
23 Prov. of Canada
24 Gore and D'Amato
25 Used more Elmer's
27 Muffin ingredient
32 Casanova
33 Live
34 Satellite's path
36 Fire-truck adjunct
39 Pro __
(proportionally)
41 Assail
43 Rice drink
44 Boat berths
46 Word before firma
or cotta
48 __ Plaines, IL
49 Vintage cars
51 Most theatrical
53 Delinquent
56 Moving vehicle
57 Carnes or Novak
58 Party time

64 On the briny
66 Put into words
67 Foil kin
68 Over there, old-style
69 Noses (into)
70 Special-interest grp.
71 Sp. miss
72 Hearing or sight
73 Witty sayings

DOWN
1 Dean of *Lois & Clark*
2 Land measure
3 Bernard or George
Bernard
4 Native of Nairobi
5 Folders
6 Pseudologist
7 Newts
8 Escapee
9 Tennis starter
10 *Wheel of Fortune* buy
11 Party time
12 Magazine unit
13 Out of vogue
21 Sailors' saint
22 Psyche segments
26 San __ Obispo
27 Gridlock causers
28 By mouth
29 Party time
30 Encourage
31 Lo-fat foods

35 Bakery item
37 ___ out a living (gets by)
38 TV sitcom *Empty* ___
40 Mimic
42 Go across
45 Cola or tonic
47 Food stabilizer
50 Morning events
52 Trousers measurement

53 Gives the nod to
54 Brim
55 ___ nous
59 Pack ___ (quit)
60 Victory signs
61 Lhasa ___
62 Take five
63 Longings
65 Periodontists' grp.

94 BUZZ WORDS

by Bob Lubbers

ACROSS

1 Ring official
4 Aroma
9 __ lazuli
14 Wallach or Lilly
15 Turkic native
16 Papas or Cara
17 Small bus
18 Solo
19 *I Remember Mama* mama
20 Orthographic contest
23 Snow __ (deception)
24 Actor Davis
25 Conducted
26 One, in Arles
27 Knicks' rivals
28 Iron alloy
31 Gratis
32 Needy
33 Sows
34 Slender at the belt
38 Watchful
40 Remain
41 Not present?
42 Helps in crime
44 Slot fillers
48 Favorite
49 Health resort
50 Eagle's nest
51 Palindromic preposition
52 Big trouble
56 "...poem lovely as __"
58 Street kid
59 "__ in my backyard!"
60 Logic
61 M. Zola
62 Single
63 Westphalian city
64 Inhibit
65 Mao __-tung

DOWN

1 Cosmetics king Charles
2 Go by
3 Best-quality
4 Passé
5 Colombian city
6 Ian Fleming's alma mater
7 Da __, Vietnam
8 Tweeter range
9 Sweetened the sod
10 Southern constellation
11 Swore falsely
12 Sang
13 U.S. Navy battalion
21 Lily, in Lille
22 Moray
28 Bribe
29 Tug's chore
30 Rub out
31 Lawyer's charge
32 L.A. clock setting
33 Pigpen

34 Horse operas
35 Garfunkel or Linkletter
36 Addams Family cousin
37 Airline to Sweden
38 Mollify
39 Hamlet's attacker
42 GI address
43 Brought by scow
44 X

45 "We __ alone"
46 Oxlike mammals
47 Sofa
49 Luster
50 *Roots* Emmy-winner
53 Application information
54 Give off
55 Ceramic square
57 Pilot's hdg.

95 SODA-JERK JARGON

by Ann Seidel

ACROSS
1 Chicago team
5 Risked
10 Stickum
14 Competent
15 Cheer up
16 Well-ventilated
17 Person, place or thing
18 Milk measures
19 Miami's county
20 Scots negative
21 Coffee
23 Jock
25 Not in the pink
26 A snap
27 Common buzzer
32 Intended
34 Office machines
35 Actress Ullmann
36 Middle of 57 Down
37 Took the measure of
38 1990s veep
39 __-de-France
40 Heptad
41 Sand ridges
42 Sewer entrances
44 Western buddy
45 Canine comment
46 One who abstains
49 No ice
54 *Uno, due, __*
55 Gung-ho
56 Clapton and Ambler

57 Turner of rock
58 Pastrami palace
59 Sinuous
60 Bitter
61 Contribute to the pot
62 Mexican moola
63 __ out (supplements)

DOWN
1 Showy tropical plant
2 German sub
3 Dose of Bromo-Seltzer
4 Sun Yat-__
5 Sheriff's aide
6 Mrs. Kramden
7 Relative standing
8 Diminutive ending
9 Foreordained
10 Irksome critic
11 Irish writer O'Flaherty
12 Pakistani language
13 Regarded
21 Topnotch
22 Corrida cries
24 Screen Turner
27 Confused feelings
28 Beasts of burden
29 Vanilla ice cream cone
30 Land of Tara
31 Nights before
32 Hurt badly
33 Big name in jazz
   singing

34 Quitting time for many
37 Popular book category
38 Wise guy
40 Classify
41 Pioneer Boone, for short
43 Finnan __ (smoked dish)
44 Balances evenly

46 Cheesy chip
47 A Muppet
48 Peruses
49 "If I __ Hammer"
50 Roaster
51 Cadence
52 Pennsylvania port
53 Smacks
57 Inventor's monogram

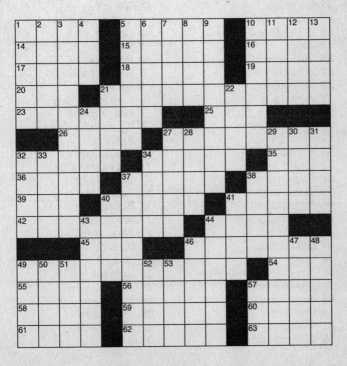

96 ACROSS THE BOARD

. . . .

by A.J. Santora

ACROSS

1 "Daniel Boone" poet
6 Where Anna was governess
10 Sweatshop?
13 __ at Eight
14 Caesar's accusation
15 Cat's dog
16 Fictional sleuth
18 Underground element
19 Yalie
20 CNN reporter
22 Adjournments
25 Extinguished
27 James and Place
28 Dud
30 __ Dawn Chong
32 Close friend
33 MA motto start
34 Loan business
37 Poker game
39 Denial word
40 Part of Q&A
41 Medicinal plants
43 Evil spirit
47 Line dance
48 Heat
51 *The Day Kennedy Was Shot* author
54 Kingsfield's profession
55 Menlo Park monogram
56 WWI-era dancer

59 Naval off.
60 Post-WWII alliance
61 Chaplin in-law
62 NC summer setting
63 Clothes line
64 Hotsy-__

DOWN

1 Official order
2 Sign up
3 Wind dir.
4 Profit ender
5 Secret meeting
6 Geisel, pseudonymously
7 Willow genus
8 "__ o'clock scholar"
9 Saki's kin
10 Making fun of
11 Mary-Louise and Sarah Jessica
12 Amaze
13 Big name in farm machines
17 What, in Paris or Madrid
21 Sins
23 Example
24 *Vidi*
26 Poor grade
28 Jacket style
29 Writer Chase
31 Sicilian city

32 Snoop
34 Most clever with words?
35 Coll. degrees
36 Not Dems. or Reps.
37 Pouch
38 Pac-10 team
42 Compartments
44 Schematically colored items

45 By swallowing
46 Stairpost
48 __ Penh
49 Fish eggs
50 Florida mecca
52 "*Dies* __"
53 Bristle
55 Placekicker's prop
57 "It's __-win situation!"
58 Stage decor

97. OINK SPOTS

by Lee Weaver

ACROSS

1 Weird
4 Declare
8 __ glider
12 Place for a rodeo
15 VIP's wheels
16 MP's headache
17 __ *Holiday* (Hepburn film)
18 Champagne bucket
19 Tortilla dough
20 Place to put coins
22 Wilbur's talkative friend
23 Hiding spot
24 Fencing swords
26 Bell or jalapeño
30 Alumnus
31 Mixed bag
32 __ and void
35 Greedy king
39 Not even once, to a poet
40 Caviar source
41 Outfit for Nero
42 Office furniture
44 Gossip tidbit
46 Colo. Springs letters
47 Leader
49 Electric current unit
51 Singer Ross
53 Norway's capital
55 Part of NWT
56 Happy place to wallow

61 Ending for young or hip
62 Alan of *M*A*S*H*
63 Home of President Bush
65 British composer
66 Oboist's need
67 63 Across, e.g.
68 Film holder
69 Top rating
70 Do lawn work

DOWN

1 Boat mover
2 Bit of rain
3 Half: Pref.
4 Excuse
5 Clergyman
6 Sign
7 Laborer
8 Got carried away on stage
9 __ of (onto)
10 Facial features
11 Delighted
13 Washed-up horse
14 Point of view
21 Sea dog's tale
25 Actress Dawber
26 Small lake
27 Robt. __
28 Some desserts
29 Government patronage source

30 Merriment
33 *Exodus* author
34 Land parcel
36 B$_{12}$ amount
37 Lab medium
38 Snugly secure
43 Junior, e.g.
45 Stag or stallion
48 African desert
50 Palace protectors

51 Raison __
52 Cara or Castle
53 Poet Nash
54 Tint
55 Ivan was one
57 Margarine
58 Dog doc
59 School test
60 Western alliance: Abbr.
64 Make a seam

98 LOOMING

by Robert W. Land

ACROSS
1 Tel __
5 Roman's 1650
9 Sounds of surprise
14 Vittorio De __
15 Like __ of sunshine
16 Kind of committee
17 Exaggerate, story-wise
19 Former Dolphins coach
20 Comedienne Coca
22 Relative of etc.
23 Transatlantic message senders
26 Polite bow
28 French schools
29 Rabbi of yore
31 Of a curved projection
32 Sired
33 Hesitant syllables
36 Ret. accounts
37 Steer
38 Take a glance at
39 Landers or Blyth
40 Manufacturer
41 Actress Sharon
42 Impelled
44 Typewriter bar
45 Update the outlets
47 Showed gratitude
48 Hot spot
49 Gere or Rodgers
52 *Endymion* author
54 *Enterprise* pace

58 Smithy's shaper
59 Sunburn balm
60 Woody's son
61 Office worker
62 Family members
63 Box-office figure

DOWN
1 Dolt
2 Celeb
3 Here: Fr.
4 Ice-cream flavorings
5 City heads
6 Hauls
7 Give a hoot
8 Actress Fontanne
9 Vapor
10 Stick (to)
11 Badminton bird
12 Negri namesakes
13 Armadillo-like
18 Arab chieftain
21 Social radiance
23 Johnson of *Brief Encounter*
24 Oak seed
25 Boxing technique
27 The nth degree: Abbr.
29 Hayes or Hunt
30 Doctor Frankenstein's assistant
32 Two-wheeler
34 Indian queen

35 Bergen dummy
37 Road worker
38 Play 'em as they are
40 Russian space station
41 Sail supports
43 2/3 of a movie dog
44 Molds
45 Cheese choices

46 Happening
47 Pulsate
50 "__ only kidding!"
51 Colombian city
53 __-mo
55 Time period
56 Wapiti
57 John or Jane

99 IN THE RING

by Bob Lubbers

ACROSS

1 Paradise
5 Cavil
9 Part of RSVP
12 Ann __, MI
14 Gen. Robt. __
15 Check out
16 What an unsteady boxer has
18 Pueblo pot
19 Inner quality
20 Consumes
21 Ballgame official
25 Asian holiday
26 Condé __
27 One who hurls
29 Lemony
31 Aunt Millie's competitor
32 Author Deighton
34 "__ boy!"
37 Ring agility
41 Linemen
42 "Oh, boy!"
43 Mitchell mansion
45 Left-turn commands
48 Cabin piece
50 Durango money
53 Owns
55 Temporary resident
56 Honolulu's home
57 Llama cousin
59 RR depots
60 Ring protector

65 Kingly address
66 Day start
67 Broadcast
68 Compass pt.
69 Not fooled by
70 Bargain time

DOWN

1 Canal locale
2 Joanne of *Red River*
3 Recede
4 __ Hill
5 Boston NBAer, for short
6 Certain Alaskan
7 Rue
8 Madrid money
9 Saucy music?
10 Ocean specks
11 Smallest
13 Pick up a lease
15 Do a 28 Down's job
17 Hardly ever
21 *Clermont*, e.g.: Abbr.
22 Abrade
23 Grinder's gear
24 Ring punch
28 Ring figure
30 Uncooked
33 Right away
35 Song syllables
36 Ohio city
38 14 Across' country: Abbr.

39 Cartoon caveman
40 Jerk rapidly
44 T-man
46 Explosive sound
47 Watering place
49 Certain tides
50 Deputized riders
51 Kitchen descriptor

52 Take part in
54 Gush
58 __ extra cost (free)
61 "__ a deal!"
62 Epoch
63 Animation unit
64 Wool-coat owner

100 ON THE RUN

by Raymond Hamel

ACROSS

1 Xavier's ex
5 Muzzle
9 Fumbles
14 Main point
15 About
16 Get __ in the face
17 Ireland symbol
18 Light gas
19 Rhône feeder
20 Company picnic competition
23 Third word of "America"
24 Broadside
25 Sea: Fr.
26 Swearing
31 White House Scottie
33 Dolly's last name
34 Made a rug
36 Ilk
38 Pimlico contest
42 Chip in
43 Apollo's mother
44 Small amount of progress
45 Phoenix suburb
47 Heartbreakers' head
49 François' friend
51 Former Delta rival
53 Inclement
54 Ten-second event
61 Bestow a gift
62 Peace symbol
63 "... wish __, wish ..."
64 Covering the vicinity
65 River to the Elbe
66 Package binder
67 Clarinetist-bandleader Johnny
68 Puerto __
69 Toledo's lake

DOWN

1 Tooth problem
2 Crow
3 Small town
4 Exile
5 Stitched without machines
6 Plays for a fool
7 Cool it
8 Pay tribute to
9 Sloop structure
10 "Back in the __" (Beatles tune)
11 Bargain place
12 Mockery
13 *Inside the Third Reich* author
21 Counting game
22 Bumbler
26 Yodeler's perch
27 Miles of film
28 Not easily perturbed
29 Mr. Coward

30 Electronic babysitter
32 Cheater's cubes
35 Last word of Missouri's motto
37 Camper's need
39 Small falcons
40 Large floppy hat
41 Piggery
46 Reverent fear
48 Walk like a dog

49 In the future
50 Saki's real name
52 Venomous bookkeeper?
55 Twosome
56 Boo-Boo's buddy
57 With, in Avignon
58 Crosby tune of '44
59 Indian wrap
60 __ Park, NY

ANSWERS

1

M	A	E		H	A	R	M		R	E	A	C	T
B	I	L	L		O	L	I	O		O	S	C	A	R
A	N	I	L	L	W	I	N	D		O	P	E	R	A
R	E	G		I	M	A	G	E	R	S		T	I	M
D	O	N	N	E		S	O	R	E		B	O	O	M
O	L	E	O			A	D	V	A	N	C	E
T	A	R	S	A	L		E	T	H	E	R	E	A	L
			T	H	A	T	N	O	O	N	E
A	P	P	R	O	V	E	D		T	I	T	L	E	S
M	I	L	I	T	I	A			T	O	P	E
O	R	A	L		S	T	A	N		B	A	S	I	C
R	A	T		C	H	A	P	E	A	U		E	S	E
I	N	T	R	O		B	L	O	W	S	G	O	O	D
S	H	E	E	P		L	E	N	A		N	U	D	E
T	A	R	D	Y		E	A	S	Y		U	T	E

2

B	L	A	N	C		A	S	P	S		R	A	T	A
R	U	R	A	L		S	K	A	T		A	L	A	N
O	N	T	H	E	S	K	I	D	S		C	A	I	N
W	E	E		R	E	E	F		A	I	S	L	E
	W	I	N	D	F	A	L	L	S
A	T	T	I	C	S			B	E	L	T	E	R	S
P	E	W	S		S	T	I	N	T		D	O	T
S	L	I	P	O	F	T	H	E	T	O	N	G	U	E
E	L	S		P	O	R	E	S		E	A	S	T
S	A	T	I	A	T	E			M	A	D	R	E	S
	F	L	O	P	O	V	E	R	S
B	O	L	O	S		M	A	S	C		A	L	T
A	L	O	U		T	R	I	P	H	A	M	M	E	R
R	E	I	N		A	L	T	O		D	O	O	N	E
B	O	N	D		U	S	S	R		E	S	S	A	Y

3

C	P	O		M	C	A	N		E	Q	U	A	L
L	A	L	L		A	R	C	O		R	U	N	T	O
A	R	E	O		L	E	E	R		R	A	D	O	N
S	T	I	C	K	L	E	R		R	A	Y	O	N	S
P	I	C	K	L	E	D	B	E	E	T	S
			O	U	T	S		Z	S	A		T	H	E
S	H	O	U	T			P	R	E		P	A	I	R
P	O	T	T	E	D	M	E	A	T	B	A	L	L	S
A	N	T	S		E	E	G		A	S	C	O	T
T	K	O		U	F	O		I	S	I	T
			S	T	E	W	E	D	P	R	U	N	E	S
A	R	T	H	U	R		L	E	A	D	R	O	L	E
C	U	R	E	R		G	L	A	D		E	V	A	N
A	L	I	E	N		T	E	T	E		S	E	T	S
T	E	X	T	S		O	N	E	S		L	E	E

4

S	A	W	S		O	N	A	N	D		P	H	A	R
A	L	I	T		S	E	N	O	R		I	O	W	A
D	Y	N	E		C	A	N	O	E		Q	U	A	G
A	N	G	E	L	A	L	A	N	S	B	U	R	Y
			L	O	R	E			S	U	E
R	O	D	E	O	S		O	M	A	R		A	W	L
A	V	E	R			B	R	I	G	S		S	H	Y
J	E	S	S	I	C	A	F	L	E	T	C	H	E	R
I	R	K		D	R	I	E	D		H	E	R	E
V	A	S		L	E	N	O		S	C	E	N	E	S
			B	E	D			S	T	A	R
M	U	R	D	E	R	S	H	E	W	R	O	T	E
N	A	N	O		N	O	H	O	W		I	K	O	N
E	X	I	T		Z	A	I	R	E		E	A	R	N
W	I	T	H		A	R	M	E	D		S	Y	N	E

5

```
H O L S T   T O M A   T A C K
A L E T A   A W O L   R I A L
L A S E R   V E T O   A D A M
  F L A S H I N T H E P A N
    E L I E     L A U D
M A Y   R A L E   C O G S
E R G   V E R E   C H O R E S
S M O K E A N D M I R R O R S
S O R E S T   G E N E   U R N
R E Y S   U E L E   N A S
    H E A P     M A D D
  F O O L S P A R A D I S E
C O O L   T I M E   D O O Z Y
H A Z E   O T I S   E N U R E
A M E S   N Y E T   D E T A T
```

6

```
B M O C   C A P E K   M E A D
R O B E   O L I V A   A L V A
A T O Z   S T A I R   L O O N
T H E A R T O F L E T T I N G
        N Y E     S E R E
P R U N E L L A   M A S H I E
L O B E   L A D D   D E A N S
A D O   S O M E O N E   S E T
T I A R A   P L E A   E T R E
E N T I R E   E S T I M A T E
    P A V E     I C E
E L S E H A V E Y O U R W A Y
L E A N   D E L O N   S O R E
M A N E   E R I K A   O V A L
S P E D   S T E E L   N E L L
```

7

```
A P E G   D A S H   U L T R A
P A A R   O L E O   S A H I B
B L U E A N G E L   S M E L L
    C R E E P E R   O G L E
A R B I T E R   E N U R E D
C A L A I S   A L L U R E
C R A N E   G R E E T   E A T
R E C S   G R E A T   A N N E
A R K   T R I A D   A R M E R
  B L O A T S   A T T A R S
S L E E P S   R E T I N A E
T E A S   P O L A R I S
R O U S E   L I L A C T I M E
A N T E S   G E L T   E L A N
W A Y N E   A S Y E   S E E D
```

8

```
R A D A R   A I D E   F C C
A R I S E   A R D E N   L A H
R O C K A N D R O L L   I N E
A O K   M E D A L   S N O W
  B A E R S   S T A T E S
R E B A S T E   C A R P S
A T O M S   S T A T I S T I C
S O U   S O S     O D E
E N L I S T E E S   F I N E S
D R A Y S   E A R N E S T
F R E O N S   A R I E S
E A R N   A M O R E   B A S
L T D   P E B B L E B E A C H
L E A   R E L E E   E N T R E
A D M   O N E R   E S S E S
```

9

```
C H A D   A S P S   S C A B S
L Y M E   L E A H   L E V E E
I D A L U P I N O   A S I D E
F R I   M I Z   O C T A V E S
F A N Z I N E S   O E R
    S A E   O V E R R A T E
S P E A K   A C I D   O K A Y
W H I Z   Q T I P S   M I R E
A I R S   U T E S   C E N T S
P L E A S A N T   F U R
    G U S   Y E L L O W E D
S A L A D I N   L A P   E P A
P L E B S   A R T C A R N E Y
C A N O E   R O O K   E D E N
A W A R D   C O N S   N Y S E
```

10

```
B A E R   S N U B   P S H A W
A C R E   I O N E   A L A M O
G H O S T G R A I L W A T E R
S E S T I N A   R A S T E R S
    U P S   P U P   T R E E
S I M P S   M U T A T E
I D O   T O T   L A R E D O
R O L L E R C O M M U N I O N
S L E E V E   U T A   R O I
  F E A S T S   A V E R T
L A I T   C T S   A L I
U T R I L L O   A N T O I N E
C O W S E E W A R O I L D A Y
I N I T S   E G A D   E I N E
D E N S E   D A T E   T O A D
```

11

```
D A Y   M A T   P O T   B C D
I D O   E L O   A B E   E L A
I J U S T B L E W I N F R O M
    A R I E L       S L A T S
T H E W I N D Y C I T Y T H E
D I N   C O O     A G O   E E L
S C O T       O N E R S
      W I N D Y C I T Y I S
      M E D E S       T E S S
E R A   P A L   B S A   R O E
M I G H T Y P R E T T Y B U T
P A L A U       A R E T E
I T A I N T G O T W H A T W E
R A S   E R E   H E I   A H A
E S S   S A M   A D S   G O T
```

12

```
I S S U E   A H S O   H O S T
T O O N E   R O A D   O R E O
C H I C K E N A N D S T A R S
H O L O   R E X   M O O L A H
      O P T     M E O N
Y A N K E E B E A N     E S T
I V I E D   E A R T H   A R A
P A N D A   A T I   A P R O N
S I N   L A T E N   S E T O N
L Y E   M I N E S T R O N E
      C O A T     O A F
C A R L O T   A D D   O R C A
C R E A M O F M U S H R O O M
V E N I   R E E D   A C T U P
I S O R   Y E N S   W E E P S
```

13

```
A G E S   S T A R   T W I N E
L E N T   L I R E   E I D E R
A T T A   O R C A   E D I T S
N A R R O W E S C A P E
S T E E L E     T R E A S O N
      D R A M   S E W A G E
T A S S   S I L O   A G R A
A R C H   S I T O N   K E E L
M O R O   H A R D   S E T S
O V E R D O   E I R E
R E S T O R E   I M E L D A
      L O N G D I V I S I O N
S P O O L   G I N A   S N U G
A R N I E   E V I L   E D G E
P E O N Y   D E T S   S A H L
```

14

```
C L E M   S A K S   E L F I N
R U N E   E T N A   R A I S A
A L I D   A T O M   O I L E D
M U D D Y W A T E R S   T R I
      L E A R     H I G H E R
R O D E N T   G L O O M Y
I D I   S E G U E   N A R E S
G I R L   R A I D S   N I R O
A N T E S   P L A T S   C I A
      Y A P P E D   R A T H E R
C A D D I E     E A S Y
A G O   G R E A S Y S P O O N
K A Z O O   M I S C   I N T O
E V E N T   I D E A   S E T S
D E N T S   R A N T   T R O Y
```

15

```
H O S T   A C T U P   S O B S
A R I A   C H E T H   C L E O
H E L P   C A M E O   H E A D
A L L E Y O O P   T A L O N
      L O S S   C O M E
S E E O U T   B L O O P E R S
A R B O R   T R I P S   L I P
R A S P   P R A M S   L I N E
A S E   B O I S E   M O O S E
H E N C O O P S   B O O T E D
      H O P E   G A M P
  S H A R D   H U L A H O O P
V I A L   E M A I L   O H N O
I D L E   C A L L A   L I I I
Z E S T   K N E E D   E O N S
```

16

```
M I D A S   R L S   Z O R R O
A B I D E   I I I   A X I O M
Z I G Z A G G E D   R I A T A
E D S   G A U G E   A D L E R
      A M P E R A G E
D E F I L E     P O S T O N
E V I L   S P R I T Z   O B I
P E R E Z   F D A   A A R O N
O R E   A R C A N A   B A T E
T Y R O N E     D A S H E R
      C Z A R D O M S
C A C T I   H A D E S   P T A
R E H A B   O Z O N I Z E R S
A R E N A   D E R   S O R E S
G O F E R   A S S   T O K E N
```

17

```
O S H A   B O A T S   D U K E
R A I N   E N S U E   A R I A
B U R N O N E S B R I D G E S
S L E E P   S T A B S   E V E
      S E W       I N N
H S T   C A R R Y A T O R C H
B E E S   R O U E     M E R E
O G L E   D A M N S   A L A N
M A L I   S O T O     D I S C
B L A Z E A T R A I L   C H E
      E A R       R U B
A W E   S C A L E   L E A S T
L I G H T A F I R E U N D E R
O L G A   D A V I S   C A N E
W E S T   E R E C T   H Y D E
```

18

```
B A I R D   P R O D   H E A L
A C T I I   H A L O   E L S E
T H E O A K R I D G E B O Y S
H E M   M E A N     P R I E S
      K O P S   M A C E
R O N N I E M C D O W E L L
F I N E D   E X I T   W A Y
L A K E   S T R I P   T I N E
A T E   V I O L     K I N D S
W A Y L O N J E N N I N G S
      I D G O   O O N A
C R E A K   S M U G   Z A G
B A R B A R A M A N D R E L L
E V I L   A N O D   O A K I E
R E N E   G A G S   M E E S E
```

19

```
D I G U P   A M A T   S I B S
O S A K A   C A L E   K N E E
J A M E S M C A I N   E T R E
O W E   T U E S D A Y W E L D
      C A S S   A N A   R E Y
H A I R   E S S   T W A S
O R N O   R E O   E N T I A
W E D N E S D A Y A D D A M S
L A I U S   P I P   E T A T
A S S T   Y E P   R E N O
A W N   A A A   L I P S
B I L L Y S U N D A Y   A L A
A D A Y   T R A I N R I D E S
C O K E   E A R N   E L E V E
A W E S   D R A G   X E N I A
```

20

```
T H O R   M E T   P E R S E
E A V E   F A L A   U N I T E
T H A T L U C K Y O L D S U N
H A L T E R S   L A S   E N S
      O E R     O R A L
M O O N R I V E R   R E P O S
I L K   E I N   A S S E R T
N D A K   S P R A T   S T L O
D E P O R T   O P T   R O N
S N I P E   C L O U D N I N E
      S L U R   N E E
A O K   I N A   F I L L E R S
S W I N G I N G O N A S T A R
K E T C H   K O N G   O T T O
A S H O T   S O D   N E S S
```

21

```
  S A C   R A J A H   P A W S
M O L L   E R I C A   U R A L
O U T O F S I G H T   S E G A
P R O S I T     A G H A S T
E S S E N   S T E R E O
      T A K E A D I M V I E W
S L O   L E X U S   E R I E
P U L L E Y   S P R A N G
A L I I   T I M O R   N E O
T U N N E L V I S I O N
      G N O S I S   P O R K Y
G E N E V A   B E C A L M
A V E R   F U Z Z Y L O G I C
L I L I   E M E E R   S A N A
E L L E   R A N D D   T S E
```

22

```
G A Z E   D I N A   S E A T S
A R I A   E T A T   I N L E T
P E P S   M E T S   E V E R Y
E A S Y C O M E E A S Y G O
      S A L     A R T
B A T T L I N G   C A T C H A
O D O R   S E A M   S H O A L
L O W E   H O M E S   E N I D
A B I E S   N E A T   B A L E
S E T T L E   S T R A I N E R
      E V A     A L G
F I V E E A S Y P I E C E S
A E S O P   R A M P   A R A T
S T A T E   O N C E   S U R E
S E W E R   N E A R   Y E L P
```

23

```
OMAR FEDS BWANA
TUNA ISAW RIGID
INON ROTA OSOLE
SINGLEPARENT
    YES MACES
SSS GIBB TORPOR
OPQ ADAMS IRAE
DOUBLESOLITAIRE
ARAL SCONE NED
SETOFF SPUR GDS
STARE NSA
TRIPLEDECKER
BABEL CORA TAXI
ADORE OMIT UNIT
MOPSY TAKE PETE
```

24

```
GOGH APTLY SHOW
ALOE TAHOE PUMA
LENA TRENT ICON
AGED IRS PEKOE
  WAIL UPHILL
FLICKA NAIL ERR
LATHE CASTE BOA
ASHE MOLDS REST
SET PARSE TERSE
HRH ARGO INGRID
  ELIXIR STAY
SOWED IGO UFOS
EMIR NASAL GIRL
RENO FREUD ENDO
ANDY LISLE SNOB
```

25

```
PANDA AGORA FDA
ORIEL PARES LOT
PEBBLEBEACH ITT
EASTON ALI ANTI
    OTTS STYPTIC
ABBR EMU AIRSEA
SAO GRAVELPIT
KRUPA LEM ELOPE
  LAVALAMPS NIA
MADDEN SAR CENT
OVERLAP SOSO
TIRE TEE OTOOLE
HAD ROCKEFELLER
ETA ALOES VEGAS
REM HESSE ERASE
```

26

```
SAGA POSH AWRY
AVES ABEE SPREE
COOTURIER OPEDS
ONLINE ELLEN
    INCS EVADE
SCUTTLE FERINE
MARTY ETATS TRA
ALOE PATTY FIAT
ROW SATES SLOGS
COMETS REPHONE
NOVAS SARA
  SOLES OMAHAS
SPOKE AUKOURANT
HOMER ASOF EINE
APED BENS ALAN
```

27

```
RAMS BEARS SCAR
ARIA OGLED TACO
GINSENGTEA AFRO
EDISON ELK LEEK
    NEAR MIA
SHAW TIE DONUTS
POPPA DREAM LAW
IMPASSE TYMPANI
TEL PASHA ALIGN
EYELET APB OTOE
  CAN NERD
SWIG BAD EASTER
LIDO MULLEDWINE
OREO OREAD ADDS
TERN CARPS NEST
```

28

```
CLAW MAST THEME
ROSA AXLE RAGES
ARTS REAL ANGLE
WRITERSBLOCK
SERENE ANT BRA
    IDES TOILES
AMEND MAJORSUIT
SELA MIO LENO
STENOPADS CESAR
ARCARO AERO
DOT ION ALSACE
  OFFICERSCLUB
AMATI NAVE ALLS
PANIC EVES MOPE
TENSE RENT STAN
```

29

```
S E M I   M I M E S   R A M S
A M E N   O N E T O   A V O N
M I S T   L U R C H   T O M E
  T H E M A R C H O F T I M E
    R A R E       R A D A R
  M A N X     A C T O N
B A B A   B A L A A M   F I E
B U L L D O G D R U M M O N D
C I E   A G R E E S   E A R S
    B R Y A N     Y A L E
E B S E N     C A A N
J O H N S O T H E R W I F E
E R A T   W H I L E   N O L A
C A P O   N A D I A   G R I N
T H E N   S T E E L   S T A T
```

30

```
S C A B   N O D E   A C A R
N O N O   K O R E A   N O M E
O D D N U M B E R S   I M U S
B A S E B A L L   T A M E S T
    L O R E   D E C A D E S
U P B E A T   M E R E L Y
R O A S T   B I A L Y   A M A
A R C S   G O L L Y   S C O W
L E K   K A R A T   B U T T E
  J E N S E N   E R N S T S
L A U R E L S   R A I D
A N D R E A   O U T C R I E S
R I G A   M A M B O K I N G S
G M E N   P R E E N   E R A T
O A S T   S A N S   D E N S
```

31

```
S P E N T   F E W   N O B E L
C A L V E   A L I   E C O L E
R U S S E L L M D   S T O L E
E L A M   A L S O   S A K E S
E A S I E R   W A I V E
    T A K E S   S E E R E D
R I G H T   T E A S   S T L O
U N A   J O E M T   W A D
T R O T   U N T O   P I A N O
H I K E R S   O R S O N
  E X I T S   H I J A C K
O V E T T   A L V A   O G L E
R E F I T   V A O H A N L O N
R I F L E   O C T   W E E S T
S N E E R   R Y E   E S T E S
```

32

```
S A R A   S A H I B   A R A M
A G A R   O C A L A   R O M E
J A C K O F A L L T R A D E S
A N E   C A D   H E L E N A
K A R A T     J E S S
    K A B O O M   C A S T E
A L T I   O T H O   U S E R S
J O H N N Y O N T H E S P O T
A B A T E   O D E R   E T T E
R O T O R   L O S E R S
    O G E E     O S C A R
O N S A L E   K I T   A G A
T O M D I C K A N D H A R R Y
I D E A   K O R E A   C R E E
S E E M   O A T E S   E Y E D
```

33

```
A S P E N   B R A D   T K O S
C A R L O   R O B E   V E I N
C H E S S P I E C E   H A L O
S L Y   E R A   S P O O N E R
    P R O N G   E N S U R E
R A C I S M   E G R E T
A L E C   O N O R   A L I A S
T I N T S   O R E   L A D L E
S E T U P   E G G S   R E B A
  R I F L E   H A R A S S
A D H E R E   I T A L Y
T R A C E R S   A R I   N E O
L A V A   B I L L I E J E A N
A P E R   E L E E   N O I S E
S E N D   R O T S   S E L E S
```

34

```
J U N T A   C O P S E   M C P
A R O A R   A B A T E   A H A
R I S K C A P I T A L   K I R
    E A T S   O Y S T E R S
A G E N D A   H I S   O B O E
D I T   E L I A S   S T E M
E V E N   O W L   S T A L A G
P E R I L S O F P A U L I N E
T I N G E S   W I N   S E C T
T A G S   A A N D P   V E T
T A L L   P L Y   B R I E R Y
O S C E O L A   B A E R
P H I   D A N G E R F I E L D
P O T   O Z O N E   A N G E R
S T Y   R A N U P   B A G G Y
```

35

T	O	S	C	A		L	I	T	H	O		E	R	G
A	M	O	U	R		E	R	R	O	L		N	O	R
C	A	P	T	I	V	A	T	I	N	G		C	P	A
O	R	S		S	I	S		P	E	A	C	H	E	S
		I	T	S	A	B	O	Y		H	A	R	P	
A	M	I	N	O		B	E	D		J	A	N		
C	O	N	V		A	L	L		C	A	R	T	O	N
E	N	T	I	T	L	E		C	A	R	M	I	N	E
S	A	R	T	R	E		T	O	Y		I	N	C	A
		I	I	I		L	I	L		A	N	G	E	R
	S	I	G	N		P	E	E	L	I	N	G		
C	O	U	G	A	R	S		E	S	T		A	L	A
U	N	I		W	E	L	L	G	R	O	O	M	E	D
D	I	N		E	L	I	T	E		N	O	O	S	E
S	A	G		S	L	E	D	S		Y	O	K	E	S

36

A	L	P	A	C	A		D	A	H		S	C	O	W
B	E	A	R	I	N		O	V	E	R	C	O	M	E
P	A	L	A	T	E		L	E	H	A	R	H	A	R
	D	E	P	A	R	T		G	E	N	R	E		
			A	D	A	N	O		S	E	W			
L	A	T	H	E		T	M	E	N		A	K	C	
O	R	I	O	L	E		A	G	E		T	U	N	A
G	O	T	H		A	B	H	O	R		O	D	O	R
O	S	L	O		T	I	A		D	E	W	I	T	T
S	E	E		E	C	H	O		T	H	O	S	E	
			C	N	N		A	L	G	A	E			
		O	T	A	R	U		D	I	G	E	S	T	
K	A	Y	A	K	Y	A	K		R	E	H	E	A	L
R	E	E	M	E	R	G	E		T	R	E	N	T	S
A	L	M	S		S	A	N		H	E	E	D	E	D

37

A	P	E	D		P	L	E	A		A	S	H	E	
C	O	M	E		R	O	A	M		B	E	T	A	S
T	U	M	B	L	E	D	R	Y		A	R	U	L	E
S	T	A	T	E	S		S	C	R	I	M			
			A	E	R	O		A	R	A	B	S		
	P	R	E	S	T	O	N		P	I	L	L	A	R
F	L	U	T	E		M	E	A	T	S		E	T	O
R	A	M	A		M	A	I	L	S		O	B	I	T
O	T	B		D	O	N	D	I		I	N	U	R	E
M	E	L	T	E	D		A	C	A	D	E	M	E	
	S	E	R	V	E		S	E	R	E				
			S	A	I	L	S		A	A	R	O	N	S
G	L	E	N	N		H	U	M	B	L	E	P	I	E
P	E	A	C	E		E	T	A	L		L	I	N	E
S	I	T	E		D	E	L	E		Y	E	A	R	

38

C	H	E	R		S	A	G	S		Y	E	A	S	
L	O	L	A		C	O	M	E	T		E	T	C	H
I	S	L	E	R	O	Y	A	L	E		L	U	R	E
F	E	E		U	T	A	H		R	E	L	I	E	D
T	A	N	G	L	E		S	A	N	T	O			
			R	E	S	T		P	E	E	W	E	E	S
H	A	G	A	R		I	M	P	S		S	A	D	A
E	B	O	N		A	D	U	L	T		T	R	I	M
A	B	E	D		L	I	M	E		M	O	N	T	E
P	E	R	C	A	L	E		S	P	A	N			
			A	L	E	R	T		A	Y	E	A	Y	E
C	A	R	N	E	Y		H	I	L	O		L	U	V
A	W	A	Y		C	R	A	T	E	R	L	A	K	E
S	E	G	O		A	B	N	E	R		A	M	O	R
E	D	E	N		T	I	E	R		D	O	N	T	

39

S	C	R	E	W		E	V	I	L		S	L	U	M
L	A	U	R	A		C	A	N	E		L	O	R	I
E	V	E	R	Y	T	H	I	N	G	T	O	W	I	N
W	E	D		L	O	O	N		O	B	E	S	E	
			T	A	R		E	S	T					
N	O	T	H	I	N	G	I	N	C	O	M	M	O	N
A	V	O	I	D		O	R	D	O		I	A	G	O
M	O	T	E		D	A	V	I	T		G	R	I	T
E	L	E	V		O	L	I	N		S	H	A	V	E
S	O	M	E	T	H	I	N	G	B	E	T	T	E	R
			U	A	E		A	N	Y					
G	U	E	S	S		E	E	R	O		C	O	B	
A	N	Y	T	H	I	N	G	F	O	R	L	O	V	E
I	D	E	A		M	E	A	T		A	I	M	E	D
L	O	S	T		P	O	D	S		S	T	O	N	E

40

D	U	S	T		P	E	L	E		A	P	A	C	E
I	N	L	A		O	C	H	S		B	A	C	O	N
A	C	E	S		M	O	A	T		J	I	H	A	D
N	U	P	T	I	A	L	S		S	U	R	E	T	O
A	T	T	E	N	D		A	T	A	R	I			
			C	E	O		A	V	E	N	G	E	D	
B	R	A	S	H		L	A	V	E		G	I	L	A
R	O	S	A		R	I	T	E	S		U	G	L	Y
A	H	O	Y		A	V	E	R		S	P	I	E	S
G	E	F	I	L	T	E		N	Y	E				
			N	O	I	R	E		E	M	B	O	S	S
M	A	G	G	I	O		A	L	L	I	A	N	C	E
I	N	U	I	T		O	R	A	L		S	I	R	E
C	O	N	D	E		A	T	N	O		R	O	O	D
E	N	S	O	R		S	H	A	W		A	N	D	Y

41

J	A	W	S		R	A	F	T	S		P	A	S	A
E	C	H	O		E	E	R	I	E		E	B	A	N
T	H	E	S	U	P	R	E	M	E	C	O	U	R	T
S	E	T		S	U	I	T		U	N	T	I	E	
			N	E	T	A	S	S	E	T	S			
L	A	U	R	E	L		P	L	O		F	B	I	
P	E	T	E		S	O	L	U	T	I	O	N		
S	E	R	V	I	C	E	S	T	A	T	I	O	N	S
S	K	I	E	S	A	R	E			D	R	O	P	
T	S	P		R	P	I		C	R	E	E	D	S	
		M	A	T	C	H	H	E	A	D				
T	E	P	E	E		A	I	D	S		F	E	Z	
I	T	S	A	L	L	I	N	T	H	E	G	A	M	E
G	N	A	T		1	0	0	0	0		A	R	I	A
E	A	T	S		P	R	I	N	T		S	E	L	L

42

K	A	P	P	A		C	O	T	T	A		I	D	A
A	L	I	E	N		O	R	I	O	N		R	A	M
N	I	C	K	E	L	O	D	E	O	N		O	L	E
			E	W	O	K		T	U	R	N	I	N	
A	C	T		B	U	S		E	L	E	C			
L	I	I		T	O	P	P	E	R		T	U	B	
A	N	N	I	E	S		I	N	S	P	I	R	E	
S	E	P	T	S		I	T	O		A	R	T	E	L
	M	A	S	S	I	V	E		T	R	E	A	T	Y
A	N	A		S	E	R	V	E	S		I	L	L	
	A	L	L	A		S	I	N		N	E	E		
W	A	L	L	E	D		A	O	N	E				
O	I	L		G	O	L	D	B	R	I	C	K	E	R
O	D	E		G	R	A	I	L		B	R	I	D	E
S	A	Y		S	E	D	G	E		S	U	D	A	N

43

D	O	F	F		I	B	S	E	N		L	A	I	T
E	L	L	A		N	O	I	S	E		O	L	G	A
B	L	A	N	K	V	E	R	S	E		S	T	O	P
T	I	M		E	A	R		E	D	I	T	O	R	S
S	E	E	M	E	D		I	N	T	O	W			
		I	N	E	R	T		O	N	E	O	F	A	
R	A	M	S		R	O	A	D		S	E	W	E	R
I	W	A	S		S	A	L	E	M		K	E	E	L
L	O	G	I	C		M	I	L	O		E	S	S	O
E	L	I	N	O	R		C	L	O	W	N			
		G	R	I	T	S		R	E	D	C	A	P	
M	A	R	L	E	N	E		A	I	L		H	A	L
A	L	A	I		G	R	O	U	N	D	Z	E	R	O
T	O	R	N		U	S	I	N	G		A	R	O	W
S	E	E	K		P	E	L	T	S		P	I	N	S

44

I	D	O	L		R	A	M	A	R		M	B	A	
T	A	M	E		E	R	I	C	A		R	O	A	N
C	L	E	F		C	E	D	E	S		I	N	S	T
H	I	N	T		A	N	D		H	O	G	T	I	E
			I	M	P	A	L	A		A	H	E	A	D
L	O	R	N	A		S	E	X	I	S	T			
E	L	I	T	E	S		O	E	R		O	B	O	E
W	I	S	H		R	I	F	L	E		N	E	N	E
D	O	K	E		T	O	T		S	H	T	E	T	L
			L	O	A	T	H	E		O	H	B	O	Y
A	N	N	U	L		A	E	R	A	T	E			
H	A	I	R	D	O		R	M	S		M	A	R	S
O	P	E	C		T	R	O	I	S		A	L	I	T
L	E	C	H		I	N	A	N	E		R	A	C	Y
E	S	E		S	A	D	E	S		K	N	O	X	

45

O	S	C	A	R		P	A	R		A	B	B	A	S
M	O	O	R	E		O	L	E		S	A	U	C	E
A	L	A	R	M		T	E	C		P	A	S	T	A
N	I	X	O	N	N	I	X	O	N		S	H	I	M
		W	A	C	O		N	E	E		B	O	A	
M	A	B		N	O	N	E	F	O	R	N	U	N	N
A	L	O	F	T		R	E	N	N	E	S			
T	A	X	I		L	I	A	R	S		S	H	E	A
	E	R	R	A	N	T		I	T	E	M	S		
G	O	R	E	I	S	G	O	R	E	D		D	U	E
O	R	B		P	E	R		A	R	I	A			
D	I	O	S		R	O	B	B	R	O	B	B	E	D
W	A	X	E	S		U	R	I		T	I	A	R	A
I	N	E	P	T		P	I	E		I	D	I	O	M
N	A	S	T	Y		S	O	S		C	E	N	S	E

46

A	S	P		P	R	E	Y		M	E	L	E	E	
G	I	R	D		S	A	R	A		A	T	O	L	L
O	N	O	R		I	F	A	M	A	N	A	S	K	S
R	E	M	U	S		T	A	T	I					
A	W	O	M	A	N	T	O	H	E	L	P	H	I	M
E	S	S		M	A	I		A	N	A	T	O	L	E
			P	O	R	E	S			E	W	E	S	
W	I	T	H	A	C	R	O	W	B	A	R	I	T	S
	O	L	A	Y			S	A	L	V	O			
M	I	L	L	D	A	M		R	O	I		A	N	S
B	E	C	A	U	S	E	H	E	C	A	N	N	O	T
			A	E	R	O		N	A	I	V	E		
L	E	V	E	R	A	L	O	N	E		I	S	E	E
A	P	A	R	T		I	K	O	N		L	E	N	D
M	I	L	N	E		N	E	W	S		S	A	S	

47

```
S A G A   B L O T     T U N A
U R A L   R E M A P   U N I T
Z E R O   I N A N E   R O P E
I N T H E B A R G A I N
E T H A N E     O N A   T R A
      S R A S   U N R E E L
I L L B U Y T H A T   O N T O
D E E R E   T A N   A S T R O
A H O Y   T A L K E D S H O P
H A N N A H   L A N D
O R A   B A A   T U F T E D
      P A Y S T H E P R I C E
A R G O   E T H E R   E L L E
R E A L   R E E S E   E D A M
M O P E   R E A D   S E T S
```

48

```
F A D   N A R C     P O L A R
I R A   A L I A S   O B E S E
J U M P S T A R T   M E S T A
I G N I T E   L E A P Y E A R
        E A R L   N B A
J E R S E Y B O U N C E
M A P   E R N O   T O R A H S
P I S A   N R A   O T O E
S L O G A N   I M A S   I L E
      M O R O C C O B O U N D
        S A L   K O L N
H E D G E H O P   R U D D E R
A L I E N   D A R T B O A R D
T I A R A   S T E E L   D O A
H A Z E L   S A D E   A S S
```

49

```
A L F A   M A X I E   S T Y
D A U N T   I C I N G   T I O
A R M T W I S T I N G   E L L
P R E S E N C E   C R E E K
T Y S   E M U   D U A L
    K N E E S L A P P I N G
L E N S   A I R S P E E D
L A L O   E R N S T   I S M S
O N E C A R A T   I N T O
B A C K B R E A K I N G
      T E S S   I T T   A R A
P A R D O   A S S A S S I N
I T O   L I P S M A C K I N G
C O N   U N I T E   T E A S E
K P S   T A C I T   E N E R
```

50

```
A B B A   S A G S     P A C S
M O O D   P L O P   P I N U P
P O O L   H A T E   U L T R A
    B R I T I S H A I S L E S
      B E N   R N A
V A G   A X I S   O N C A L L
A L I A S   T I E R   O D E A
P L A N E S O F A B R A H A M
O I N K   A N T S   E L O P E
R E T A R D   S T A G   C T R
      E A U   L I P
P R I N T S O F W A L E S
M O O R E   A R I A   A X L E
I N T O W   I T T Y   Z E A L
T E E N   R O S S   A S P S
```

51

```
S E A   A C R A B   A P A R T
H U N   M O O R E   P I P E R
O R I G I N A L S   I E R E I
T O T E   S N E E R E R
A P R O N   S T A C C A T O
T E A R O S E   V E E J A Y
    G L U C O S E   B O I L
  S E A N C O N N E R Y
H A U L   L E P A N T O
A T E A S E   P A T S I E S
J A Z Z E S U P   A N N I E
    E C S T A S Y   A L L E
E V E N T   I N T E R N E E S
L I M B O   L A I T Y   T E T
S A T Y R   E Y R I E   S N O
```

52

```
A P B S   A T E S T   A H O Y
M A L E   V I L L E   C O V E
B R O W N I E M I X   O M E N
I D O   C A R   M A T R O N S
T O M C A T   L E N I N
    H A R T E   S E S A M E
C A R O   I R O N   S Q U A T
U P U P   X E N O N   U N T O
T E M P S   K A T E   A T T N
E X P E L S   R E A R S
    D A T E D   T O H O L D
T R U M P E T   D N A   N E E
R O S E   P U R E E D P E A S
I D E A   O D O R S   B A S K
P E S T   N E O N S   A L E S
```

53

B	U	S	M	E	N		P	S	S	T		M	A	T
O	N	T	I	M	E		A	L	O	E		A	R	I
W	I	L	L	I	A	M	W	E	L	D		I	L	L
			S	T	R	I	P	E		S	A	T	E	D
S	R	I			L	A	P	P		S	A	N	E	
W	E	N	D	E	L	L	W	I	L	L	K	I	E	
I	N	S	U	R	E	S			N	A	Y			
G	E	T	O	U	T			T	R	I	O	D	E	
			P	T	A		S	E	I	S	M	A	L	
	W	A	L	T	E	R	W	I	N	C	H	E	L	L
S	E	R	A		R	E	I	N			N	E	E	
H	A	R	M	S		O	N	E	T	W	O			
I	S	O		W	A	L	T	W	H	I	T	M	A	N
N	E	W		A	G	A	R		O	R	I	O	L	E
E	L	S		T	R	E	Y		M	E	S	S	E	D

54

T	U	L	I	P		A	R	C	H		P	A	N	T
A	F	I	R	E		L	A	R	A		O	L	I	O
R	O	C	K	B	O	T	T	O	M		P	O	L	O
A	S	K		B	R	O	S		S	E	Q	U	E	L
			L	E	S			E	T	T	U			
G	R	E	B	E	S		S	P	E	C	I	M	E	N
R	O	V	E	S		B	A	E	R		Z	E	N	O
A	S	I	A		F	A	D	E	S		Z	E	R	O
P	S	A	T		A	B	A	S		G	E	T	O	N
H	I	N	T	E	D	A	T		T	U	S	S	L	E
			H	O	D	S		J	O	T				
Y	E	M	E	N	I		H	E	E	L		B	A	S
E	V	E	R			S	O	U	L	S	E	A	R	C	H
N	I	N	A		T	A	L	L		S	H	A	R	E
S	L	O	P		S	T	A	Y		S	A	T	E	D

55

B	L	T		L	E	M	U	R		F	A	R	A	D
O	O	H		A	M	I	N	O		A	R	I	S	E
O	N	E	T	O	U	C	H	O	F	V	E	N	U	S
	G	R	O	S			I	D	I	O	T	S		
A	B	E	T		S	E	T		B	R	E	E	D	S
P	O	T		T	E	N	C	H			R	O	E	
T	W	O	F	O	R	T	H	E	S	E	E	S	A	W
			E	M	I	R		T	U	R	F			
T	H	R	E	E	F	A	C	E	S	O	F	E	V	E
I	R	E			P	A	R	I	S		T	I	X	
M	E	S	S	E	S		T	O	E		R	O	V	E
		O	C	T	A	N	E			M	O	N	A	
F	O	U	R	H	O	U	R	S	T	O	K	I	L	L
R	E	N	E	E		M	E	T	R	O		A	D	E
A	D	D	E	R		B	R	E	A	D		N	I	X

56

F	A	D	S		P	E	C	S		F	A	B	L	E
A	L	O	E		O	R	A	N		E	R	R	O	L
R	E	N	T		M	I	R	O		N	E	A	P	S
G	R	A	H	A	M	C	A	R	A	C	A	S		
O	T	T		S	E	A	T	T	L	E		S	T	A
			A	T	L			A	S	T	E	R	N	
H	A	B	L	A		T	E	A	M		A	R	A	N
O	S	L	O	B	O	A	T	T	O	C	H	I	N	A
S	H	I	N		N	I	C	E		L	O	E	S	S
T	O	N	G	U	E				S	A	E			
S	T	D		R	A	V	I	O	L	I		T	U	T
		D	U	B	L	I	N	D	E	M	N	I	T	Y
A	M	A	N	A		E	D	I	E		A	M	I	N
E	A	T	E	N		R	U	S	T		T	E	L	E
R	E	E	S	E		S	E	T	S		O	R	E	S

57

W	E	A	N		C	R	E	E		C	H	I	L	D
E	R	D	A		H	O	A	X		H	O	V	E	R
L	A	M	A		E	A	R	T	H	I	N	E	S	S
S	T	I	C	K	E	R	P	R	I	C	E			
H	O	T	P	O	T			A	T	A		P	C	T
			C	A	L	F		A	G	L	A	R	E	
R	U	S	H	H	O	U	R		O	A	S	I	S	
G	U	S	T		S	E	R	O	W		L	E	C	H
A	N	A	I	S		B	L	U	E	B	O	O	K	
P	O	G	R	O	M		S	E	R	A				
E	N	E		M	A	O		E	S	K	I	M	O	
			F	E	N	D	E	R	B	E	N	D	E	R
M	I	C	R	O	N	E	S	I	A		O	A	T	S
P	R	E	E	N		T	A	L	C		T	H	R	O
G	E	O	D	E		S	U	L	K		S	O	O	N

58

T	O	B	E		B	L	A	B	S		C	A	S	S
O	N	Y	X		R	O	S	I	E		A	T	I	T
R	U	T	H		A	C	T	O	N		R	A	T	A
O	S	H	A		C	H	I	L	D	S	P	L	A	Y
			E	L	I	T	E			L	E	E	R	S
O	R	B	I	T			R	A	G	O	U	T		
R	O	O	N	E	Y		S	A	V	E		N	A	P
S	M	O	G		A	M	P	L	E		C	O	M	O
O	A	K		K	W	A	I		N	E	R	V	E	S
			S	I	L	I	C	A		T	E	E	N	Y
S	L	O	P	E			V	O	C	A	L			
W	E	L	L	V	E	R	S	E	D		M	I	L	T
A	N	D	I		D	E	T	R	E		E	D	I	E
S	T	E	T		I	D	E	S	T		R	E	N	E
H	O	R	S		T	O	N	E	S		Y	A	K	S

59

S	A	T	I	N		A	N	T	S		A	O	N	E
I	L	O	N	A		N	O	R	A		I	V	A	N
F	L	U	S	H	E	D	W	I	T	H	R	A	G	E
T	A	R	P		A	S	I	S		A	W	L	S	
		A	P	R		T	O	G	O					
D	O	W	N	I	N	T	H	E	D	U	M	P	S	
U	N	A		A	S	H	Y		D	E	A	R	E	R
D	E	L	L		E	I	N		N	I	N	A		
S	A	L	O	O	N		N	A	P	S		D	O	C
	L	A	C	K	I	N	G	B	R	A	V	E	R	Y
			K	A	T	Y		E	L	I				
	H	A	S	P		L	O	S	E		E	A	S	E
D	E	V	O	I	D	O	F	K	N	O	W	H	O	W
A	L	O	U		I	N	M	Y		R	E	E	S	E
M	I	N	T		I	S	E	E		A	R	M	O	R

60

C	A	P	R	A		P	I	E	T	A		S	I	S
H	I	R	A	M		O	N	E	A	L		E	S	E
A	D	O	B	E	G	I	L	L	I	S		S	O	V
		F	I	N	A	L	E			B	A	B	E	
A	D	O		P	U	T	T	Y	W	O	M	A	N	
T	O	R	T	E	S		R	A	I	D	E	R	S	
L	O	M	A	N		L	A	I	R	S				
	M	A	C	A	D	A	M	A	N	D	E	V	E	
			M	E	T	A	L			O	V	A	L	S
U	K	U	L	E	L	E		E	M	A	I	L	S	
V	I	N	Y	L	E	X	A	M	S		N	A	T	
A	M	I	S			C	A	T	K	I	N			
L	O	T		G	U	N	I	T	E		I	R	E	N	E
U	N	E		A	N	O	D	E		L	A	S	E	S
E	O	S		T	O	N	Y	S		N	E	S	T	S

61

O	R	A		O	P	T	S		S	T	R	I	F	E
M	E	R		K	E	E	N		H	O	O	V	E	R
A	B	E		A	T	S	E	V	E	N	T	E	E	N
H	U	S	K	Y		L	E	O		O	A	S	T	S
A	S	I	A		W	A	R	R	A	N	T			
		X	R	A	Y	S		T	R	E	E	T	O	P
S	T	E	N	O		D	E	E		W	P	A		
W	H	E	N	I	M	S	I	X	T	Y	F	O	U	R
H	E	E		I	A	M		H	E	A	T	S		
Y	A	N	K	I	N	G		S	A	N	T	O		
		I	N	G	E	S	T	S		A	T	O	M	
M	A	R	S	H		S	A	P		S	L	A	V	E
O	N	E	M	E	A	T	B	A	L	L		N	O	R
T	A	V	E	R	N		L	U	A	U		G	I	G
S	T	A	T	E	N		E	L	S	E		O	D	E

62

C	A	S	T		T	A	P	A		L	O	O	T	S
R	U	L	E		O	V	E	N		U	N	P	I	N
O	D	I	N		B	I	S	T		N	E	E	D	I
W	I	N	E	T	A	S	T	I	N	G		N	E	T
D	O	G	T	A	G				Y	E	A	H		
			R	O	S	C	O	E		R	O	W	S	
W	O	W	E	D		P	U	N	T		E	U	R	O
A	R	R	A	Y		R	R	S		C	A	S	E	S
S	L	A	G		Y	A	L	E		U	S	E	N	O
H	Y	P	E		O	Y	S	T	E	R				
		P	R	A	Y			R	I	A	T	A	S	
E	P	A		C	O	S	T	U	M	E	B	A	L	L
G	A	R	B	O		P	A	R	I		H	U	L	A
A	L	T	E	R		I	R	A	N		O	P	E	C
D	O	Y	E	N		T	A	L	E		R	E	E	K

63

C	L	A	P	S		S	T	E	A	M		D	O	C
R	O	B	O	T		O	H	A	R	A		O	N	A
O	V	E	R	E	X	P	O	S	E	D		W	E	N
W	E	L	T	E	R		R	E	A		A	N	O	N
			L	A	P	E	L		L	L	A	N	O	
S	T	U	B		Y	E	A		S	I	G	N	E	T
L	A	P	A	Z		R	U	S	T	L	E	D		
O	B	T	R	U	D	E		P	E	A	B	O	D	Y
	H	O	N	E	S	T	Y		C	R	U	E	T	
S	C	E	N	I	C		O	R	B		A	T	A	D
P	A	C	E	S		C	R	I	E	D				
H	U	R	T		K	O	P		T	E	E	T	H	E
E	S	E		U	N	D	E	R	A	C	L	O	U	D
R	A	E		S	E	E	D	S		A	I	R	E	D
E	L	K		P	E	R	O	T		L	E	N	Y	A

64

I	N	N	S		S	A	L	T		B	O	B
N	E	A	T		A	R	E	A		E	T	A	T
S	U	P	E	R	B	O	W	L		L	I	C	I	T
A	T	O		K	I	O	S	K		I	C	K	E	S
N	E	L	S	O	N		I	V	E		S	S	A
E	R	I	C		S	P	E	E		S	T	I	R
		A	W	A	K	E		R	A	T	O	N	
	A	M	E	R	I	C	A	S	C	U	P		
	T	E	P	E	E		A	L	E	T	A		
S	A	R	I		N	O	N	E		R	A	S	P
O	H	O		S	A	M		A	R	T	F	U	L
T	I	B	E	T		A	D	O	B	E		L	I	I
S	T	I	L	E		H	O	M	E	P	L	A	T	E
I	C	E	R		A	N	A	T		A	M	O	R
S	E	N		S	O	N	S		H	E	R	S

65

```
M O V E   B L E E P   A P E D
U R A L   O U T R E   V O L E
F I L I B U S T E R   A P S E
T O E   A N T E   J A S P E R
I N T E N T     R U N T Y
    L A Y O V E R S   C A W
A W F U L   L O V E   D O G E
T H U D   C I G A R   I C E D
M E R E   O V U M   M A K E S
O W L   S L E E P S I N
  O A T E R     A M A Z O N
A M U S E S   S E M I   I D O
J A G S   L A N D S C A P E S
A C H E   A M I N O   C U T E
R E S T   W O T A N   E P O S
```

66

```
L A M A S   E R R O R   O L A
A D O R E   L E A F Y   N O R
M O O L A   M E W T A T I O N
    V E N D E D   N O O S E
P L A N   D R I P S   O N E S
L A B   S E S T E T S   Y R S
O I L O N     S L A P S
P R E P A I D   T R A I N E E
    T I R E S   I D E A L
P A P   L A N O L I N   I S I
A R I D   S T R A W   A G E S
D O L E D   T R O U G H
R U F F R I D E R   N O S E D
E S E   U S U R Y   I N A N E
S E R   G L E S S   T Y L E R
```

67

```
C O O L   S H O R T   F A W N
A C R E   T U D O R   I S E E
P A L M S U N D A Y   N E A T
E L O   I N K   C O U G A R S
T A V E R N   C H U T E
    L E I G H   T E R R O R
C R I B   N O A H   S L O P E
L O G O   G O R E S   A S I A
A V O W S   F I R E   K E E P
M E R G E D   O R A T E
    R E A C T   S E S A M E
S A L E R N O   Y O N   C O B
P L E A   G R E E N T H U M B
I O N S   L A T T E   A T M E
T E T E   E L C I D   M E A D
```

68

```
A S A P   G R A M   S I S A L
G A R R   R E N O   C A P R I
O S L O   O A T S   U N I T S
G H O S T W R I T E R   R E A
    I R E S     A V A I L S
N E S T E R   D I V E S T
I M P   E S S E N E   H A H A
L I E N S   H E T   S E W E D
E L E E   M O R O S E   A R E
D E R I D E   P L A Y O N
H I D D E N   M A E S
A D E   W I N D O W S H A D E
T A M P A   I R O N   R O O K
C H O I R   N O S E   A N T E
H O N E D   A P E D   M E S S
```

69

```
S A Y S O   B R A T   D A M S
S M O T E   E E R O   O P E C
T O N E D   N A I R   T A D A
    M I L D M A N N E R E D
M O E   P A S S   A O R T A S
U N L O A D   A D O S
S I M P L E S I M O N   A T M
K N E E   A V E   A L O E
Y E R   E A S Y R A W L I N S
    B R I E   R A B B I S
A F F A I R   T A C T   I C Y
P L A I N C L O T H E S
T A U T   O U S T   R O M A N
E R N E   O R C A   E L I T E
D E A D   L E A R   D O Z E D
```

70

```
S T A T   C O C A   S P I L L
A U D I   A L L S   P A R E E
S L A G   S L A T   A N S O N
S I G H T S A W R O N G
  P E T R I   O B I   M A E
    S I N E S   O S M O N D
F R A   B I T T H E H O O K S
I O N A   T I A   E R L E
F I G H T S A L I A R   E E L
E L I S H A   E R N I E
S S E   I R A   A D L E R
    G R A D E T H E M A I D
T A M E S   A L O E   E D D Y
A V A S T   M I N I   R I G A
P E T T Y   S E E M   S E E N
```

71

```
ROME  TROT  CISCO
EVEN  OAHU  AMMAN
BANGUPJOB  SPARE
ATLANTA ALIASES
GEORGE  CLINCH
   DINER  TOTHEE
NEWER MADE  SIDE
UPI  DRIVERS TIL
LEST ELIS  COSTS
LEERED  NISAN
  CURING  TRENTA
TORNADO LOANERS
ROADS BOOMBOXES
ONCLE LAMP  TUNE
NAKED ETAS  ESTS
```

72

```
HARPO  ACES  CSA
ONEOF PLODS  HAJ
FASTFRIENDS  ABA
FIE EASED  CRUX
ASTORIA   OATH
  RUNNINGWATER
SLEEP  VERONICA
EEK  SPIRO  NOT
TIESCORE  EAGLE
HASTYPUDDING
  LOSS  UNTAPED
TOJO  SANKA  ILO
ONA QUICKSILVER
NEZ BLAHS  LEONE
YAZ SENT  SITIN
```

73

```
STAT  SLOT  STILT
ARLO  PAAR  CORER
BOAR  RITA  ANAME
UNIQUETECHNIQUE
  USE  REA  IRS
ROPES   GRASS
IRA  STOOGES
OBLIQUECRITIQUE
  REBATES  RAN
  THEDA  BASRA
WIA  RAT  LIL
ANTIQUEBOUTIQUE
IDARE GOAT  GULL
SERAI INRE  NINA
TRINI SESS  SPAN
```

74

```
SMOLT  QED  MATTE
HANOI  URE  ALOHA
ALONG  AIL  RIMES
HEREHERE  BYEBYE
   TET  BOSN
LOUIELOUIE  STEP
APRONS  KART  RNA
SEGUE  OAS  OMITS
TRE DIOS  MOPPED
SADE  THERETHERE
   DAIS  HAH
WINWIN  WELLWELL
ILIAD BAS  EERIE
LITRE TRU  SAGAN
LEEDS UPS  SLOMO
```

75

```
DOER  SLAB  GABLE
AGRA  NOLO  ALOOF
FLIPFLOPS  MAMET
TENTO MOOSE  BBS
  OLE  METES
MAGRITTE  REDHOT
ERR CHANCE  GERE
ROOS  ELTON  ELAN
ISUP REEKED  LTD
TENURE  RELEASES
  DREAM  YIP
ADZ ALIBI  GAFFS
AREAS LEMONTREE
HARPO ALAN  HEEL
SWORN NAME  YELL
```

76

```
MOHAIR  PORTENT
ADORNER AVERTED
CORONAS REBATES
KRAMERVSKRAMER
   ARS  EAT
TICS  ALS  MUTTS
AVA CALF  BIGBEN
HOPEAGAINSTHOPE
ORELSE MEAT  NEA
EYDIE FAD  SEEK
   PUG  BOA
CREMEDELACREME
POOLING ASHTRAY
FINANCE STERILE
CLANKED ERECTS
```

77

```
HARM WIDE  BODES
ELEE AKIM  OPERA
LAIR LOSE  TIERS
LINCOLNCENTER
ONSIDE  OREL
     ITS    RESETS
SEDAN  HEADSTART
OMAN  TOONS  UVEA
BITTEREND  IDEST
SLEEVE   YES
    ANAT  REPAST
   MIDDLEAMERICA
LEAVE  DELI  OMAR
ALTER  ANON  VALE
BLESS  SATE  ETES
```

78

```
MALTS  LAIT  FEET
SCOOT  IBID  OGLE
SIRFRANCISDRAKE
 DEFINED  OGDEN
      DEN  CARE
HEBREW  DUCKSOUP
OLIOS  PARTY  SPA
OBOE  BINDS  USER
POT  FONTS  BRINK
SWANLAKE  BLEEDS
   OUZO  SRI
ARGON  SNIGGER
WILDGOOSECHASES
ECOL  SATE  TITAN
DAME  USSR  SNELL
```

79

```
ADUB  TIDE  MIST
SALE  LOOS  OLEOS
HUNNICUTT  NLERS
 BAIO  OROURKE
  GOBI  PALS
REYNOLDS  HOOKER
ENO  ALKI  GRADE
SOUL  HEINZ  YSER
ALLAT  SMEE  EMU
WALKER  PERELMAN
  ELIE  DOMO
SIMPSON  MGRS
ATOOT  JAZZYJEFF
OHARA  OTIS  ABAB
 ENTR  YOGA  MAXI
```

80

```
BIRD  BIBB  ALVA
IVIES  ALAR  LAID
BANTU  RENO  INCA
INDEPENDENTSDAY
   REL  TUTORS
ATA  REVISER
PERE  CORE  OLLIE
EXECUTIVESWEETS
STAUB  LIMA  STOP
OPENSUP  ANY
SHOFAR  DII
CAPITOLGAINSTAX
AGES  POLL  CLEAR
PART  EVIL  HEARA
ERAS  REBA  TREY
```

81

```
MARGE  CHAT  LEND
AGAIN  RAMA  LIEU
SHIRT  ELEPHANTS
CANARDS  SIAMESE
   FEATS  OVA
EIFFEL  INCA  PMS
LORE  INDIAN  HIP
STASH  ALL  AVILA
IAM  ENVIED  ULAN
ESE  LIEN  ORLONS
   LEG  GLOAT
SPOONED  AMPULES
KANGAROOS  IRATE
ISLE  ISIT  NEWTS
TOYS  AILS  ESSES
```

82

```
 EBB  STAGE  ACTI
ACRO  PILAF  KEEN
CHARGEDAFFAIRES
LEV  ICE  FORMA
ALUMNI  TERI  MEN
SORA  MOW  TAHITI
SNAP  ETES  NOCAL
   PENTECOST
OATEN  STAR  AIDS
HARRIS  ETC  INRE
MAI  STIR  HARDEN
 VALET  LAS  OSS
PRICEWATERHOUSE
REAR  ELAND  ABED
YALE  DODOS  FTS
```

83

```
A J A R   S E M I   A B E S
M I L A   I D O L   D E L L A
O M E N   N I N E   D A V I S
K I C K B A C K S   S T E M S
      R I T E   G U T S Y
  P A G E   S E R A P H
S O L O N G   S O P   E M M A
P I V O T E D   B E R R I E S
A S A N   N A B   D E A R T H
  S P I N E T   A P E S
  B A T H E   M I S C
T E R R A   P U N C H B O W L
E R R I S   U S M A   O K R A
D R A K E   R E A L   L I E N
  A Y E S   E D N A   T E N D
```

84

```
C O L T   M I M E   S A B I N
A P I A   A M O R   I L E D E
D I N G A L I N G   M I L L E
E N E   L A N K   N O B L E R
T E N S E D   I R O N I C
      C R Y   S O R E   U L M
A S C O T   C H A T   B R I E
J O H N S O N   S H E L V E S
A L I E   M O R T   N E E D S
R O M   S A T E   B O N
    I T C H E D   A U D R E Y
G E N E R A   C O N G   O B I
A L G A E   T O L L H O U S E
E L I S E   I A G O   E S E L
L A N E S   S T A N   R E N D
```

85

```
H E D G E   A A R P   W A V E
A L E U T   S H O E   A V I V
T E N T H   S E C R E T I V E
H E Y   I T E M S   M U S E S
    A S C O T   G I S
R E C U S E   B E R L I N E R
A B C D   N E L L I E   E M O
G O E S   A T E A M   M A A M
E L S   M I A S M A   E R I E
D I S T I L L S   C A N A L S
    H A S   P E R O T
S T E A M   H O R D E   H I C
T E R M I N A T E   N E A T H
A L O E   A U T O   D A N T E
B E S S   P L O P   T U D O R
```

86

```
P A C   S I N E W   D A K A R
E L Y   A D E E R   I M A G E
E L M   V I O L I N S O N T V
R A B B I   S A C
S H A R O N   S T R E A M S
    L A R O S A   C R E A T E
B A S   T A X I   N O R A S
I L I A C   A P O   S N A G S
C O M B O   R O T E   C E E
S H O U L D   T A R A W A
A N G L E R S   A D O B E S
    A N A   D O O N E
C H E R R Y C E L L O   U T E
A E R I E   E L L E N   N E D
B L E N D   R I D E S   D R Y
```

87

```
H A H A   B E A C H   A R O W
I G O R   A T B A Y   L E A H
N E W T   T H E R M   L A K E
E N D   W H O S O N F I R S T
S T O R I E S   B E E
    Y A R D   B R O A D W A Y
S T O N E   F L O O R   H I E
W O U K   B R I S K   D A D A
A D D   P A U S E   W A T E R
M O O R I N G S   M A R S
    A L I   F A C T U A L
W H E R E S W A L D O   P R O
R O V E   H O V E R   O D O R
A B E L   E R I C A   D O M E
P O N Y   D E S K S   S C A N
```

88

```
B A G S   A G A V E   A B U T
O S L O   P E T I T   M A K E
T H E U N T O U C H A B L E S
H E N N A   B E A D I E S T
    D I M S   N O T
E S P   L O W E R   L I F E R
S E E P   C A M E   P O E M E
S T A R S K Y A N D H U T C H
E A S E L   Z I T I   S E E A
S T E V E   E L E C T   D E B
    A E C   R E O S
C O G I T A T E   M A L T A
H I L L S T R E E T B L U E S
A L E E   H U L K Y   A B E T
D Y E D   Y E S E S   D E M I
```

89

```
GROSS  ALOAD  KGB
NAVAL  VALUE  HER
ARUBA  ENDTO  ANA
REMELT  ASH  SKIT
    ROBB  COOTIES
THERMAL  URGE
HORA  RAPT  LEVER
EMITS  DEL  ELOPE
MONTH  ERAS  GLEE
LEAR  SPOUTED
ILIESCU  SEMI
BAND  UND  DETACH
SUE  FINES  RAMIE
ERR  ITEMS  TROTS
NAT  BYRON  ASSES
```

90

```
OER  ADDS  STASH
MIA  SPOIL  WASTE
ARC  PANDAMONIUM
RECRANK  NEO
OUTIE  GASTON
SMOG  CYL  THETOP
HANS  OAKS  ETTU
ENT  THO  EAR
DIEM  HERA  ARTS
ALUMNI  SLA  KLEE
ARCANE  ACTII
RDS  TRIMMED
ACHORUSLION  IDA
DRANO  EGEST  TIM
SINEW  NESS  SEE
```

91

```
SCRIMP  SAFEST
IRONORE  GETOVER
LABORER  REWRITE
TWENTYONE  ATLAS
ODE  TRY
ADD  UNEASY  FOAL
TRIOS  TORTILLA
BADNEWS  WEEVILS
AMNESIAC  LEVIS
TATE  GEORGE  EEO
ITS  LOA
ROUGH  SEVENTEEN
ARCHERS  ELASTIC
SALTSEA  SINATRA
PLAYED  CAREER
```

92

```
SAPS  PLAID  ACHE
ABEE  RIATA  SHEA
HITTHESACK  HEAR
IDAHOS  HONEST
BEL  RES  TINT
INTHEBAG  NEV
DIBS  SAFE  ELUDE
ENOLA  SRA  LETIT
COXAL  TEND  ASTO
ORS  FRAMEUPS
CHIA  DNA  JET
COYEST  ALCOVE
DARE  CASEWORKER
OVEN  AKITA  EENS
MESA  LEROY  ERTE
```

93

```
CASK  CLEFS  AMID
ACHE  RIFLE  NASA
IRAN  EATER  ASST
NEWYEARSEVE  QUE
ALS  REGLUED
CORNMEAL  ROUE
ARE  ORBIT  SIREN
RATA  SETAT  SAKE
SLIPS  TERRA  DES
REOS  STAGIEST
OVERDUE  VAN
KIM  ANNIVERSARY
ASEA  UTTER  EPEE
YOND  PRIES  ASSN
SRTA  SENSE  MOTS
```

94

```
REF  SCENT  LAPIS
ELI  TATAR  IRENE
VAN  ALONE  MARTA
SPELLINGBEE  JOB
OSSIE  LED  UNE
NETS  STEEL  FREE
POOR  SEEDS
WASPWAISTED
ALERT  STAY
PAST  ABETS  TABS
PET  SPA  AERIE
ERE  HORNETSNEST
ATREE  GAMIN  NOT
SENSE  EMILE  ONE
ESSEN  DETER  TSE
```

95

```
CUBS  DARED GLUE
ABLE  ELATE AIRY
NOUN  PINTS DADE
NAE  BUCKETOFMUD
ATHLETE   ILL
  EASY HONEYBEE
MEANT FAXES LIV
ALVA  SIZED GORE
ILE  SEVEN DUNES
MANHOLES  PARD
  ARF  NONUSER
HOLDTHEHAIL  TRE
AVID  ERICS TINA
DELI  LITHE ACID
ANTE  PESOS EKES
```

96

```
 BENET SIAM  SPA
DINNER ETTU  PAW
ELLERYQUEEN  ORE
ELI  SUSANROOK
RESPITES  OFFED
ETTAS   MISFIRE
  RAE PAL  ENSE
 PAWNBROKING
STUD  NAY  ANS
ARNICAS   DEMON
CONGA  PRESSURE
JIMBISHOP  LAW
TAE  IRENECASTLE
ENS  NATO ONEILL
EST  SEAM TOTSY
```

97

```
ODD   AVOW  HANG
ARENA LIMO  AWOL
ROMAN ICER  MASA
 PIGGYBANK MRED
  LAIR EPEES
PEPPER   GRAD
OLIO NULL MIDAS
NEER  ROE  TOGA
DESKS ITEM USAF
 BOSS  AMPERE
 DIANA  OSLO
TERR  HOGHEAVEN
STER ALDA TEXAS
ARNE REED STATE
REEL AONE  MOW
```

98

```
AVIV MDCL GASPS
SICA ARAY ADHOC
SPINAYARN SHULA
 IMOGENE  ETAL
CABLERS  CURTSY
ECOLES  HILLEL
LOBAR BEGAT ERS
IRAS PILOT SCAN
ANN MAKER STONE
 DRIVEN SPACER
REWIRE  THANKED
OVEN  RICHARD
KEATS WARPSPEED
ANVIL ALOE ARLO
STENO SIBS TAKE
```

99

```
EDEN  CARP  SIL
ARBOR ELEE CASE
RUBBERLEGS OLLA
  NATURE USES
SCORER TET NAST
THROWER  TART
RAGU LEN  ATTA
 FANCYFOOTWORK
ENDS  WOW  TARA
 HAWS PINELOG
PESO HAS TENANT
OAHU  ALPACA
STAS MOUTHPIECE
SIRE MORN STREW
ENE  ONTO SALE
```

100

```
ABBE HUSH MUFFS
CRUX ASTO ASLAP
HARP NEON ISERE
EGGANDSPOONRACE
  TIS RAM MER
AVERMENT  FALA
LEVI WOVE SORT
PREAKNESSSTAKES
ANTE LETO  DENT
MESA  TOMPETTY
AMI TWA  BAD
HUNDREDYARDDASH
ENDUE DOVE IMAY
AREAL EGER CORD
DODDS RICO ERIE
```